D1622527

MY MORNING ROUTINE

MY MORNING ROUTINE

How Successful People Start Every Day Inspired

BENJAMIN SPALL and MICHAEL XANDER

PORTFOLIO / PENGUIN

Portfolio / Penguin
An imprint of Penguin Random House LLC
375 Hudson Street
New York, New York 10014

Copyright © 2018 by Benjamin Spall and Michael Xander

Illustrations © 2018 by Elisabeth Fosslien

Most Portfolio books are available at a discount when purchased in quantity for sales promotions or corporate use. Special editions, which include personalized covers, excerpts, and corporate imprints, can be created when purchased in large quantities. For more information, please call (212) 572-2232 or e-mail specialmarkets@penguinrandomhouse.com. Your local bookstore can also assist with discounted bulk purchases using the Penguin Random House corporate Business-to-Business program. For assistance in locating a participating retailer, e-mail B2B@penguinrandomhouse.com.

Library of Congress Cataloging-in-Publication Data

Names: Spall, Benjamin, author. | Xander, Michael, author.
Title: My morning routine : how successful people start every day
inspired / Benjamin Spall and Michael Xander.
Description: New York : Portfolio/Penguin, 2018. | Includes
bibliographical references.
Identifiers: LCCN 2018005893 (print) | LCCN 2018007140 (ebook) |
ISBN 9780735220287 (ePub) | ISBN 9780735220270 (hardcover)
Subjects: LCSH: Successful people—Case studies. | Habit—Case studies. |
Morning customs—Case studies. | Success—Case studies.
Classification: LCC BF637.S8 (ebook) | LCC BF637.S8 S6485 2018 (print) |
DDC 646.7—dc23
LC record available at https://lccn.loc.gov/2018005893

Printed in the United States of America
1 3 5 7 9 10 8 6 4 2

For Audra,
my reason for waking up in the morning

—BENJAMIN

For my beloved family

—MICHAEL

CONTENTS

Have you ever woken up in a panic at 8:00 A.M., bleary-eyed, with barely enough time to down a cup of coffee and get dressed before you have to get out the door? Have you ever looked at successful people and thought to yourself, "What are they doing that I'm not? How can I gain greater control of my life, like they have?"

For most of our adult lives—Michael in Berlin, and Benjamin in London—our mornings would follow this same pattern: we would roll out of bed and straightaway fall into the trap of checking our phones, email, and any notifications that happened to pop up overnight before rushing out the door for work. The underlying stress of these mindless mornings fed into workdays of fluctuating moods and haphazard productivity. Far from feeling accomplished after a long day of work, we felt exhausted, and not at all excited to repeat the whole process the next day. Does this sound familiar?

The way you spend your morning has an outsized effect on the rest of your day. The choices we make during the first hour or so of our morning determines whether we have productivity and peace of mind for the rest of the day, or whether it will clobber us over the head. Unfortunately for most of us, good days don't happen by accident. Unforeseen events will step forward to challenge your best-laid plans. If you don't dip into your inner reservoirs of energy, focus, and calm first thing, you won't stand a chance. Start your morning with intentionality, and you can then bring these "wins" with you into the rest of your day.

> "In the morning, alone in my office without interruption, I can write more in the first couple hours of the day than I can throughout the entire next twelve hours."
>
> —NICK BILTON, AUTHOR AND JOURNALIST

Since launching the My Morning Routine website five years ago, we have conducted interviews and extracted data from the morning routines of hundreds of successful individuals around the world. We quickly noticed that more and more of us are waking up to the idea that there is a better way to start the day than rushing through our precious few morning hours. What we discovered as we got deeper into the process of interviewing people about their morning routines is that almost *none* of the world's best and brightest leave their mornings to chance. This is not a coincidence!

Alongside the collective wisdom of our growing archive of more than three hundred interviews, this book contains sixty-four morning routine interviews featuring a cast of characters from retired U.S. Army General Stanley McChrystal to three-time Olympic gold medalist Rebecca Soni to the president of Pixar and Walt Disney Animation Studios, Ed Catmull to the life-changing tidying-upper herself, Japanese organizing consultant Marie Kondo. We'll share with you the surprising similarities among these routines, as well as the innovative improvisations many of these individuals made.

Some routines are all about early morning exercise and spartan living; others are more leisurely and self-indulgent.

From sleep patterns and dietary preferences to electronics use and workout rituals, we'll give you a wide range of possible practices to try at home.

WHY HAVE A MORNING ROUTINE

The point we're making in this book is not that there's one right way to start your day. We want you to experiment until you've formed a morning routine that works for you—one that makes you feel awake, alert, physically and mentally healthy, and psyched up to have a great day, even if you're not a morning person, you're a parent of young children, or you have a demanding full-time job that requires you to wake up at the crack of dawn.

The little things we do, day in and day out, impact our growth and shape who we are. In the words of John Lennon: "Life is what happens to you while you're busy making other plans." What characterizes us often starts with what we do unconsciously—and that starts with our morning routine.

Truth be told, it's difficult to have a good day without starting your morning with intention. Your mornings are a blank slate, an opportunity to start again. Even if your first action upon waking is simply going to the bathroom, this forms the beginning of a habit stack—a series of linked actions. Waking up triggers you to go to the bathroom, which triggers you to brush your teeth, which triggers you to put on your workout clothes, sit down to meditate, or put the kettle on to begin brewing your favorite cup of tea or coffee. Much like a Jenga stack, habit stacks are only as sturdy as their foundational blocks. Starting your day by checking your phone can trigger a less productive series of actions. What's more, it's harder to build a good habit stack from scratch in the afternoon, since our willpower is worn down by the stresses of the day. We're less reactive in the morning—as we've not yet spent our whole day making decisions—so we can think more clearly and be proactive about our morning.

Whether you're the chairperson of a Fortune 500 company (you can find the morning routine of the chairman of the Vanguard Group on page 56), the head of a thriving media empire (page 95), the creator of one of the most successful comic strips of all time (page 163), or anything in between, having a positive, focused, and calm morning routine can make the difference between achieving your goals and falling short of the mark.

> "Find a routine that works for you. Do not feel pressured to adjust to other people's standards of what your morning should look like. Be flexible and know when to pivot to make things as simple as possible for yourself."
>
> —SHAKA SENGHOR, LEADING VOICE ON CRIMINAL JUSTICE REFORM

Your morning routine will and should be adjusted throughout the seasons of your life. After reading this book, you will be in control of these changes; they will be deliberate and in accordance with your deepest values and your changing priorities. We will teach you how to craft the pillars of your morning routine while providing you with ideas and inspiration for what to add to or subtract from it over time.

Assuming there's some consistency in what you do first thing upon waking, you already have a morning routine whether you're aware of it or not. (Most of us mindlessly drift from bed to phone to fridge to work.) This is your starting point. Now let's create a more positive routine that works for you.

BUT I'VE NEVER BEEN AN EARLY RISER

We were recently asked in an interview whether you "have to" become an early riser to succeed professionally and be happier in your daily life. Our answer then, as it is now, is *absolutely not!* This is the most common misconception about what we do, and about morning routines in general.

> "I care less about my wake-up time than about the number of hours slept."
>
> —RACHEL BINX, DATA VISUALIZATION EXPERT

Whether you're an early bird or a late riser (or somewhere in between), your morning doesn't begin until you wake up. This may be at 6:00 A.M. or it may be at 6:00 P.M., but regardless of when it is, you'll always have that first hour or so upon waking. Your morning sets the stage for the rest of your day. That doesn't mean you have to get up early: it does mean you should use your morning to do what's most important to you.

If you're in a relationship there's a reasonable chance that one of you is an early riser while the other is a night owl. Benjamin is married to a night owl. From this he soon realized that mornings are not a one-size-fits-all situation, and that just because he's wide awake in the morning (and can barely keep his eyes open past 10:00 P.M.), that doesn't mean the same is true of his wife. Having a sleepy wife is not the same as having a sleepy baby, but it sure upset his morning routine all the same. If you face the same situation in your relationship, embrace these differences (and head over to our Adaptation chapter for more on this).

HOW TO READ THIS BOOK

In the pages that follow, each of the morning routines featured have been sorted into chapters, with each chapter focusing on something that is related to (or can help in) the formation of a morning routine. We cover everything from how to add elements such as working out, meditation, and unintimidating self-care rituals to your routine, to how parents can adjust their routine to fit in with the needs of their kids, to how to stick to your morning routine over the long haul.

While each of the routines within a particular chapter will draw on the themes of that chapter, each routine can be read as a stand-alone interview. You can open up the book and read from where you land, or choose a routine to read from the contents. For a larger overview of our takeaways, check out each chapter's *Over to You* section to get tips and suggestions to try out in your own routine.

We use the word "routine" in a positive light. To us, a morning routine isn't a monotonous series of drills you drag yourself through at the beginning of the day. Not only can the repetitive nature of a morning routine be comforting, it can function as a reminder to do the things you actually want to do.

"When you come up with a morning routine, understand that you're undertaking it in order to do something good for yourself, not to meet some stranger's standard of productivity."

—ANA MARIE COX, POLITICAL COLUMNIST AND CULTURE CRITIC

Though this book centers on interviews with people on how they spend their first few morning hours, you don't have to replicate a specific routine that we feature in full. Use each and every routine in this book as inspiration for your own—we often find something new to try out in the morning routines we publish on our website—but ultimately your morning routine is exactly that: your own. We encourage you to make the most of your routine and to recognize that the end goal isn't the routine itself, but rather the happiness and productivity it can bring to your life. Remember: You don't work for the routine; the routine works for you.

Our hope is that you use this book—part instruction manual, part someone else's diary—both as a handbook on how to create (and stick to) a positive, focused, and calm morning routine, and as a flip-book of inspiring stories. Reading these interviews affords keyholes into the most beautiful, private moments of our day. They form a patchwork study of who we are and how we live.

Let's get started.

CHAPTER 1

GETTING UP

How to Move from Your Bed to Your Morning

WHO NEEDS AN ALARM CLOCK
WHEN YOU HAVE A DOG

Waking up in the morning may be at the very top of your list of least favorite things to do, but it is, unfortunately, essential to starting your morning routine.

Deafening fire alarms and cumbersome roommates aside, there are few things that will wake you up as fast and fully as having a morning routine that you love and can't wait to get started on. With that said, sometimes we need a little push to get ourselves over the line (or rather, out of the bed) and to fully wake ourselves up in the morning.

In this chapter we'll speak with (among others) the president of MIT, L. Rafael Reif, about how he spends his first few hours upon waking; the executive director of the American Society for Muslim Advancement, Daisy Khan, on how the month of Ramadan brings a big change to her mornings; and economist and author Tyler Cowen on his unique take on breakfast (smoked trout and cheese, anyone?).

CAROLINE PAUL

Author of *Lost Cat*, former firefighter

When you're a creature of habit, and you're in no rush to change.

What is your morning routine?

I set an alarm for anywhere between 6:00 and 6:30 A.M., depending on when I get to sleep. I need sleep, but I need to wake up early more, or my day feels shot.

Next I make coffee, feed the milling animals, grab two protein bars, and sit down to read. Not the newspaper, though I do often check the headlines, but a real, honest-to-God book. If one's not around I will settle for the *New Yorker*. It's a sacred time for me, because reading has always been a part of my life and it's hard to find time for it. As a writer, it's also a vital part of my work. At this time, my partner, Wendy, is still asleep, the doggie has gone back to bed, one cat has gone outside, so there are only two other animals to contend with, one a cat and she curls up on my lap, and the other my own rambling mind, and we both stay there until the house stirs and comes to life. I have to say that the transition from the world being mine to the moment it seems to splinter and everyone wakes up—phones ring, emails come in, the dog reappears—is always jarring.

How long have you stuck with this routine? What has changed?

I've started my day with the same meal and coffee (Peets French roast, one large cup, so strong you could probably eat it with a spoon) for almost thirty years. Gosh, that's sort of embarrassing, seeing that so starkly on paper. But that consistency first thing grounds me, and sets me up to be able to handle whatever is thrown my way.

When I was a firefighter I didn't read in the morning, and I was a little looser about my wake-up time because you never knew how much of the night would be spent working at a fire or on medical calls, and I'm useless without sleep.

When I became a full-time writer and had to make my own schedule I became adamant about setting the alarm and getting up. I needed the structure, and I needed to start back on whatever book I was writing before the morning slipped away. People think that when you work outside of an office you can sleep in and how glorious that must be, but to me that's the road to discombobulation and dismay.

Have you always used an alarm to wake up?

Always. I've tried to train myself to wake up without one because it seems like a cool superpower, but I spend all night thinking about whether I'll wake up, and the anxiety isn't worth it. Once the alarm goes off, I sort of doze, but I have a dog and two cats who have heard the alarm and stare at me until I get up. It's called the animal snooze button.

What time do you go to sleep?

I would love to go to bed by 9:00 P.M. every evening. I'm just not a night person. Once the sun goes down I think, huh, not much to do anymore, and I sort of begin to look forward to the next morning already.

How does your partner fit into your morning?

Wendy's best work (she's an illustrator) is done at night, so she doesn't value her mornings like I do. This works because

I get my quiet morning and she gets to sleep without me tossing and turning.

Do you also follow this routine on weekends?

I like to get up early no matter what, but I may not set the alarm, in deference to Wendy. If I'm writing on a Saturday or Sunday, though, then I set the alarm like it's a weekday.

What happens if you're traveling?

When we travel my bag is always overweight because it's got maybe two pants and two shirts and then thirty protein bars, five books, and a bag of coffee. Wendy will say, "Caroline, it's NEW YORK CITY, they have everything!" But, nope, I'm not going to leave my morning routine to chance. Wendy is much more loosey-goosey with her days. She used to pester me to lighten the load, but it's been nine years and she doesn't bother anymore.

JAMES FREEMAN
Founder of Blue Bottle Coffee

When your old espresso machine gets you up in the morning and helps you make your most important decisions.

What is your morning routine?

I get up at 6:00 A.M. most days, unless the babies get me up before. I have an alarm clock with no snooze bar, so I can't be tempted to hit it. I have an old espresso machine (a late 1970s La San Marco Leva) that is set on a timer, so when I wake up the machine has been warming up and is at optimal temperature for making coffee.

After I get up, I make a cappuccino for me and a café au lait for my wife. I'm less optimistic before I have coffee, so my general rule is not to make any important decisions before I have it.

If I'm lucky, I have ten to twenty minutes to chat with my wife and read the *New York Times* in bed as we drink our coffee. Sometimes the dog needs to go out during this time and I have to be okay with it.

I leave for my workout at around 6:45. Post-workout, I shower, eat breakfast, feed and dress the babies, dress myself, and hop in the car. I usually have a playlist in mind for the drive to Oakland. I used to listen to NPR but it just got too depressing.

How long have you stuck with this routine? What has changed?

Several years. As we add babies, my mornings get more hectic, but so far everyone is getting what they need.

Do you do anything before bed to make your morning easier?

The kitchen is always cleaned and the house tidied before we go to bed. It's hard to fit it in but it's gratifying to wake up to a peaceful environment.

How soon after waking up do you have breakfast?

I eat breakfast when I get back from my workout. Usually a yogurt and fruit smoothie, or just yogurt, jam, and chopped raw almonds. My favorite yogurt is an organically certified, full fat, Jersey milk yogurt from Saint Benoît.

Do you have a morning workout routine?

Four days a week I do a boot camp in San Francisco's Golden Gate Park. It's exhausting and arduous and clears my mind like nothing else I've ever done. The teacher gives the impression of never wanting to be anywhere else doing anything else, which is quite rare, in my experience.

Do you use any apps or products to enhance your morning routine?

Is a coffee maker a product? Pajamas? A nice robe? Maybe I'm just too old but I don't believe that one's life can be hacked; it can only be lived.

What are your most important tasks in the morning?

Once I get to work, I try to concentrate most deeply on the people or problems that are in front of me, so, in that sense, my most important task prior to arriving at work is to arrive with a clear head and a pleasant attitude.

What happens if you're traveling?

I travel with a coffee kit so I can have control over making coffee. I have an app on my phone that I use to do an interval workout if I am away from San Francisco. Running in the parks and neighborhoods of great cities when I travel is a pleasure. I try not to schedule myself too early when I'm traveling so I can fit in a coffee and a run each morning.

ANDRE D. WAGNER
Artist, New York City street photographer

When your creative job requires you to be "on" all day long.

What is your morning routine?

I usually wake up around 6:00 A.M. to have some silent time to myself. I also keep a journal, so some days I'll write.

When I'm not photographing for hire, I'm usually out the door by 7:00 or 7:30 with my camera in hand, ready to enjoy the day. My routine changes from time to time, but I always wake up early. The morning is by far my favorite time of day. As a street photographer, I'm always engaging with people, watching people, walking all day, and being fully stimulated all at the same time. Days become full and draining. It's important that I get some quiet time to myself; it helps me stay balanced in such an emotional city.

When I'm working on photo projects I will adapt my routine to it. Two years ago when I was working in a photo studio, I would leave my house at 7:00 because I wanted to photograph in the subway for an hour or two before I had to be at work. Now that it's summertime and the light is so beautiful when the sun is rising I like to get out and take advantage of it.

Do you do anything before bed to make your morning easier?

I'm a neat freak and I like everything to be clean. Waking up to a clean apartment is the absolute best. It keeps my mind clear.

Do you have a morning workout routine?

Two or three times a week I'll ride my bike to Prospect Park and do a lap or two. It's great because there aren't many people out yet, and the park is pretty quiet. My favorite is in the fall, when we start to get that brisk morning air.

How about morning meditation?

Waking up in a clean apartment, beautiful light shining through my windows, and Miles Davis playing is my meditation.

When do you first check your phone?

I'll check my phone before I leave the house, but I try not to check it while I'm in bed. When I'm waking up I like to keep a space for my own thoughts and ideas. Sometimes there's nothing, and that's totally fine. On occasion, I'll think of something that will add to a project I'm working on, or just reflect on something that impacted me, whether an interaction from photography or just a personal exchange. When I wake up, checking my phone is not a priority of mine.

L. RAFAEL REIF
President of the Massachusetts Institute of Technology (MIT)

When staying on top of the news feels like a full-time job.

What is your morning routine?

I set my alarm for 6:00 A.M. but I rarely get to hear it—I almost always wake up around 5:00 or 5:30 on my own.

The moment I wake up I drink a glass of water, then I check my email. As MIT is global on so many levels, I try to stay current on what's going on around the world, and I want to know what happened overseas during the night. I'll try to respond to any urgent messages right away, then I take my phone or tablet to breakfast and read the news while I eat.

After breakfast I shower, get dressed, and then I'm off to my first meeting of the day.

What time do you go to sleep?

I try to go to bed around 11:00 P.M. I always read something, a magazine or a book, before lights out. I start reading that week's edition of the *Economist* on Saturdays, and that lasts me for a few days. Then I'll move on to a book for the rest of the week. I love reading history books and biographies; it's fascinating to look back at what happened, why it happened, and who made it happen.

Do you do anything before bed to make your morning easier?

Before I wrap up for the night, I look at the next day's schedule to see what my staff has gotten me into over the next twenty-four hours!

I use a fitness/sleep tracker. It tells me how many hours I slept and the quality of my sleep. It's a curiosity more than anything else. I love data, and I love comparing what the data says about my rest to how I think I slept.

How soon after waking up do you have breakfast?

Once I've responded to any urgent emails from overnight, I go downstairs for breakfast. My wife usually wakes up around the same time and joins me. We both read the news while having breakfast and comment to each other on the issues of the day.

What happens if you fail?

If I don't have a chance to check my email, I worry about what I'm missing. (Even when I do check my email, I still worry!) And it happens rarely, but if I miss breakfast for some reason, it throws me off for the whole day. The word "grumpy" comes to mind.

DAISY KHAN

**Executive director of the American Society
for Muslim Advancement**

When Ramadan wakes you up for dawn prayers,
and you go back to sleep on a full stomach.

What is your morning routine?

My wake-up time depends on the fluctuating prayer time (I adjust my wake-up time accordingly). Ramadan is a month when the body, soul, and mind not only get challenged but transformed as well. This Ramadan is really tough; I sleep at midnight, wake up from my deep sleep at 3:15 A.M. to eat a meal (*suhur*), then I finish my dawn prayer and go back to sleep on a full stomach at 4:30, only to wake up again at 8:30 to go to work.

How soon after waking up do you have breakfast?

I have to maintain an alkaline diet, so I drink lemon water right after getting up. I'll then eat a very healthy breakfast about two hours later, because I skip lunch. I start with black tea with milk (an English-breakfast variety), cooked fava beans (protein), cucumbers, arugula, or eggs, with gluten-free bread and homemade jams (made by me).

What are your most important tasks in the morning?

Getting dressed is a task because I have to dress for both work and evening events. I don't have the time to read the entire *New York Times* on a daily basis, so I scan the paper, reach for my scissors to cut out the articles I want to read, and save them in a pile for weekend reading. Every morning I feel like I'm doing arts and crafts.

Do you also follow this routine on weekends?

I don't want a routine on the weekend. That's my relaxing time. I let my body conquer me; I sleep when I am tired and wake up without an alarm.

What happens if you're traveling?

I frequently travel internationally, often finding myself on long flights, so I use sleep aids to stay refreshed in different time zones. When I'm away from home I give up my lemon water routine as it's too complicated to explain to TSA why I'm carrying lemons in my carry-on.

TYLER COWEN

Professor of economics at George Mason University, author of *Average Is Over*

When you have a hard stance against people
who shower in the morning.

What is your morning routine?

I wake up around 6:30 or 7:00 A.M., drink some mineral water, munch on a green pepper, along with cheese and smoked trout, and then I head to my laptop to check the news, email, and Twitter. Toward the end of that sequence I read four newspapers.

That entire process can take up to two hours. It prepares me to think about what I will be writing during the rest of the day. From 9:00 to midday is my main writing period, though I'll sometimes get some in after lunch, too.

How long have you stuck with this routine? What has changed?

Since way back when there was no Twitter, and I ate Spelt Flakes. But I barely remember those days.

Some mornings I bite into some dark chocolate—it needs to be 70 percent or higher, but below 88 percent—before the green pepper. I consider that a weakness of will, since the chocolate is more appropriate at the end of the sequence. The kind of cheese varies, but I prefer creamy goat cheese in the morning, or high-quality cheddar, even though those are not the best cheeses for later in the day.

What time do you go to sleep?

Eleven twenty-six P.M. Not *every* night at 11:26, but a fair number. Sometimes, if my wife and I see that it is 11:26 P.M., we joke that it is time to sleep. And then we sleep.

Do you do anything before bed to make your morning easier?

I leave my glasses on my laptop. I make sure I've already showered. Too many people waste some of their most productive morning time showering. Showering relaxes you and calms you down—why should that happen in the morning? I prefer to enjoy my shower during the evening, when I know I'm winding down in any case.

What and when is your first drink in the morning?

Gerolsteiner sparkling mineral water, an Austrian brand. First, last, and only.

How does your partner fit into your morning?

I read the papers standing next to her, and we chat interspersed with that. There is no conflict in the overall match of routines, as she needs to get out to do work of her own.

Anything else you would like to add?

The value of a good sofa and stereo is very high.

TIM O'REILLY
Founder and CEO of O'Reilly Media

When poems, philosophy, and plank pose
help wake you up in the morning.

What is your morning routine?

I normally wake between 5:00 and 6:30 A.M., rarely later. I roll out of bed and immediately do the plank for two minutes. I have a mostly torn rotator cuff, and this strengthens the muscles and helps keep it from tearing further. (I find that if I don't do this first thing, I often miss coming back to it.) I'll follow this with ten or fifteen minutes of stretches, which I do on the floor of the library next to my bedroom, in the presence of books that I love—old and new friends whose spines stimulate memories of their contents and the conversations they sparked about the nature of life and this world.

I generally prefer not to open my computer or phone until I've spent some time in the real world, so I usually putter around the kitchen for a while, making tea for myself and my wife, Jen, and emptying the dishwasher. After that, we'll usually go out for a three-mile run or to an exercise class. When

I get back, while cooling off, I let the chickens out into the yard and hang up the laundry on the line, if I've done any overnight. Then it's a shower and on to the work of the day.

How long have you stuck with this routine? What has changed?

The laundry and the love of morning chores have been part of my life for decades. The plank became part of my routine about four years ago, and the regular morning exercise with Jen is something we only got really serious about a few years ago.

The most delightful thing I've added to my routine over the past couple of years is that every day while out on my run I try to find a flower to photograph. It's amazing how many different blossoms there are, and when you look for a new one every day, you see the changes of the seasons, the immense bounty of nature, and the beauty of things that you might otherwise pass by.

I remember reading many years ago in one of C. S. Lewis's parables about a man who, after death, is walking along a road and realizes that the flowers simply appear like colored blobs to him. He is met by a spirit guide who explains that this is because he'd never really looked at them when he was alive. I don't want to make that mistake. Poems and philosophy and the way they can infuse the ordinary work of the day and the world we live in with meaning are an important part of my mental toolbox, and my meditation.

What time do you go to sleep?

Anywhere between 9:00 and 11:00 P.M., usually by 10:00. Jen and I usually play a round or two of Boggle before bed, and I like to read a bit. Right now, I've just finished the first of Upton Sinclair's eleven-volume series of novels about a character named Lanny Budd, the novels of which George Bernard Shaw said, "When people ask me what has happened in my long lifetime, I do not refer them to the newspaper files and to the authorities, but to the novels of Upton Sinclair."

Do you have a morning meditation routine?

I remember a talk given by Joseph Campbell (author of *The Hero with a Thousand Faces*, and many other books about mythology and religion) late in his life. He was in his eighties but still strong and graceful. He told the story of how Alan Watts had asked him, "What kind of yoga do you do, Joe?" He said he replied, "I underline passages." For me, the best meditation is to try to be present in every moment, and to open the doors and windows of the mind to let the universe in.

Do you answer email first thing in the morning?

Once I open my computer, I do check email. I respond to as many as I can right away, add others to a to-do list, and still others, alas, slip from my ken and are lost as they scroll off the screen. To people I meant to get back to, I apologize.

How does your partner fit into your morning?

We do most of our morning routine together, though she tends to check her devices while I start puttering in the kitchen. When I start unloading the dishwasher, she joins in. Whoever gets downstairs first starts the tea.

OVER TO YOU

"The morning is a sacred part of the day. I love new beginnings—my mother always told me not to worry, because tomorrow is a new day. I remember being little and going to sleep so excited to begin again."

—DENA HADEN, AWARD-WINNING ARTIST

Ready to get the better of your deep desire to stay in bed in the morning, ease the process of waking up, and enjoy all the moments thereafter?

"After years of trial and error, I've found that the first thirty minutes of my day have the biggest impact on how I feel for the rest of my waking hours."

—MOLLI SUROWIEC, FITNESS INSTRUCTOR

The tips you'll find below come from more than five years of interviewing people about their morning routines, with those we spoke with ranging from hard-core morning people to people who, much like all of us at some point, want nothing more than to hide their heads under the pillow when they hear their alarm. We hope you find something of benefit in what they have to say:

EXPERIMENT WITH YOUR WAKE-UP TIME

Why do you get up at the time you do every morning? Do you always wake up at the same time, or does it change depending on the day of the week or on how you feel?

For many of us, the time we get up is dependent on when we need to be at work, school, or elsewhere. Although waking up at the last minute to make it out the door on time is an okay strategy if your only goal is to avoid being fired or flunking out of class, you're going to have to experiment with waking up earlier if you want to allow more time in your day for a morning routine.

Starting tomorrow, consider getting up just five minutes earlier than usual. If you usually wake up at 7:00 A.M., set your alarm for 6:55 instead. Then get up at this new time every day for the rest of your working week (and weekend, if you wish). This may sound like a slow exercise, but adding in small changes like this makes it easier to form a new habit. Once you've been waking up five minutes earlier for about a week, add another five minutes to your experiment, so you're now getting up ten minutes earlier.

Eventually, if you keep moving your wake-up time five minutes earlier every week, you'll find a time that works for you. But keep in mind, you don't want to have a wake-up time that's so early that you're falling asleep by the middle of the afternoon.

GET A DOG (SERIOUSLY)

If you struggle to wake up in the morning, there are two solutions that are guaranteed to exponentially improve your odds:

1. Having a baby

2. Getting a dog

While we're all for the first solution, depending on your situation in life, we already have a whole chapter dedicated to the morning routines of parents. So that leaves us with getting a dog. As art director David Moore encapsulates perfectly: "It's difficult to oversleep when you have two dogs that love you to death."

If you've ever had a dog, you'll know what we're talking about here. Dogs will not let you sleep in and miss their morning walk; you're all they have, and they will not rest until you're up and enjoying the morning with them.

MAKE YOUR BED

Making your bed in the morning is one of the simplest things you can do to help wake up your mind and get you ready and prepared for the day ahead. It also reduces your chances of climbing back into it.

Social worker Heidi Sistare notes: "When the bed is made I feel like my world is clean and orderly and I can focus all my attention on my work." Making your bed can do this for you. It's one of the reasons why the military insists on soldiers making their beds every morning; it instills a sense of discipline and planning into the day.

Making your bed may not have as instantly dramatic effects as it does for those men and women who serve, but it will help set up your day in a more focused and productive manner.

SWITCH OUT YOUR BACKGROUND NOISE

If the first thing you do upon waking up in the morning is switch on the morning news (or indeed, if your alarm turns on your local radio station), we recommend cutting this out as soon as possible. These programs are stressful, and while they may indeed be keeping you informed, they're a highly negative influence on your morning.

Take a leaf out of director of the Federal Judicial Center in Washington, D.C., Judge Jeremy Fogel's book: after getting the newspaper and making a cup of coffee in the morning, he puts on some quiet classical music. "Listening to the kind of music I do—my favorites are Bach, Handel, and the baroque-era composers—almost always has a calming effect [on my morning], and the structure of the music seems to engage my attention."

TAKE YOURSELF OUTSIDE

Get some sunlight on your face and fresh air in your lungs. Go for a run or for a bike ride, or simply walk up and down your block or around your neighborhood. If you can't seem to fully wake up indoors, there's no point in lingering around—get outside. (For more on forming an exercise routine, see our Morning Workouts chapter.)

In the words of endurance athlete Terri Schneider: "I can usually be out the door within ten or fifteen minutes of getting up. I don't try to hurry, but I just don't see the point in lingering. I love the quiet and stillness of early morning, so I am motivated to get up and out in it—to feel like I have the place to myself before the rest of humanity stirs."

START YOUR MORNING WITH GRATITUDE

Shaka Senghor told us that: "The very first thing I do [in the morning] is focus on gratitude and on three things I'm thankful for. I practice gratitude on a daily basis."

When you start your morning routine with gratitude, getting out of bed will become that much easier, as your day is instilled with meaning beyond what is on your to-do list.

If you're religious, you may wish to say a prayer. Former art director Erin Loechner told us: "I start my morning with a simple prayer: Lord, help me see. That's it. Nothing fancy. I find it offers me the precise amount of perspective I need throughout the day—I'm always repeating it in my head."

DO USE AN ALARM, BUT DON'T HIT THE SNOOZE BUTTON

Most people rely on an alarm to wake up. We use them ourselves. But we can't promote hitting the snooze button, as it often brings us more harm than good.

Of course, that doesn't mean this is an easy habit to break. Teacher Richard Wotton explained: "I impose a self-ban on the snooze button; ten minutes extra sleep won't help me in the long run. In the winter, as the temperatures go below zero, this policy is pushed to the test."

The reality is that while setting an alarm is necessary for most people with full-time jobs and other responsibilities, snoozing your alarm (even if you set the initial alarm earlier, to build in time for your snooze) will often cause you to feel much worse once you finally get out of bed, as opposed to getting up the first time it sounds. In the words of writer Gray Miller, after you hit the snooze button: "Lying there pretending to sleep is like having my engine revving without ever putting it in gear." Or, as entrepreneur and former *Survivor* contestant Gregg Carey puts it: "Responsibility for life seems to be a good driver to get out of bed."

Leave Your Alarm in Another Room

If there's one change to your morning routine that will make the biggest difference to how fast you get up in the morning, it's leaving your alarm in another room. This practice has come up time and again in our conversations, and it's no surprise why.

When you leave your alarm (which, let's be honest, is often our phone) in another room overnight, the physical act of getting up and out of bed to turn it off is often enough to wake you up and get your blood flowing. As young adult (YA) author Lindsay Champion tells it: "There's no point in hitting snooze and going back to sleep if you're already standing up and fifteen feet away from the bed."

REVERSAL

There is a subsection of people who take issue with our rallying cry against the snooze button. If you've been a lifelong snoozer, and it works for you, then we don't oppose you keeping it up. Illustrator Eli Trier notes of the snooze cycle: "There's something about that nebulous half-awake, half-asleep state that I find really powerful. I often find that the solutions to any problems I've been struggling with come to me in that state, and I get insights and ideas like nobody's business."

Of course, just because you feel okay getting up after hitting snooze five times doesn't mean you wouldn't appreciate the improved energy and productivity a no-snooze rule might bring. But if you find inspiration in the half-awake state, you can get away with making your own rules.

On that note, if you've found effective methods of waking up that we haven't mentioned above, also keep these up. We recommend keeping devices outside of your bedroom overnight, so you don't get sucked into checking the social media carousel in the morning, but some of the people we spoke with for this book had different views on this topic, such as general partner at GV (Alphabet Inc.'s venture capital arm) M. G. Siegler, who told us: "I often think I should wait until I'm fully awake [to check my phone], but the truth is that checking my phone helps me wake up as it gets my brain going."

Whatever you do, don't feel guilty about your morning routine. Every disciplined professional we spoke to ad-libs a little.

CHAPTER 2

FOCUS AND PRODUCTIVITY

How to Be More Productive in the Morning

There is enormous power in putting your first few morning hours to use on your most creative and fulfilling projects, making large strides on goals that would otherwise have sat on the back burner, and feeling a sense of early morning productivity that you can then take with you into the rest of the day.

We encourage you to create a to-do list the day before and place your most important work at the top—and aside from urgent events that genuinely can't be helped, to stick to it. Be proactive in the morning instead of reacting to events that are outside of your control.

In this chapter we'll speak with (among others) Gregg Carey on the four essential components of his morning; author and contributing writer for the *New Yorker* Maria Konnikova, on why the morning is her time to say "I got stuff done" before moving into the rest of the day; and senior editor of *Fortune* magazine Geoff Colvin, who forces himself to do the most important items on his to-do list every morning, but who confesses that, despite his best efforts, he does not bat 1.000.

RYAN HOLIDAY

Author of *The Obstacle Is the Way*

When you get so much done in the A.M.
that the P.M. serves as extra credit.

What is your morning routine?

One of the best pieces of advice I've gotten comes from Shane Parrish.* It's simple: If you want to be more productive, get up early.

So I get up around 8:00 A.M.† and I have one other simple rule: Do one thing in the morning before checking email. It could be showering, it could be going for a long run, it could be jotting some thoughts down in my journal. It's usually writing. Most mornings I try to write for one to two hours before I start the rest of the day (and the to-do list I made the day before).

I shower, get ready, and head downstairs to my office/library to sit and write. The way I see it, after a productive morning in which I accomplish my big things, the rest of the day can be played by ear. It's all extra from there.

How long have you stuck with this routine? What has changed?

Routines are an iterative process. You add and adapt them

---

* Our interview with Shane can be found on page 53.

† "Early" is subjective. Like Ryan, wear your wake-up time with pride, regardless of when it is.

over time. I have been doing some version of this specific routine for nearly eight years.

I'm about four years into my current routine—each routine is slightly different depending on where I live. I think where routines get tested is as you get busier, as more opportunities come up, can you stick to it, can you resist the temptation to descend into chaos—and also, when you travel, how quickly can you come back to it. I think I'm pretty good at this. I can always be better, but I'm addicted to routine, so it is easier.

Nothing disrupts a routine like having a kid, so when my wife and I became parents I was prepared for some major shifts. It's still roughly the same—I take the baby for an hour in the morning to let my wife catch up on sleep, and in that time I sit with him and play. He sits in my lap while I write in my journal. I'll hold him while I go let the chickens out. Sometimes I will read to him. It's just a nice, slow, and peaceful addition to the routine.

The "no email in the mornings" rule has also had a big impact in recent years. It means I'm not starting the morning behind the ball. Instead, I start with wins. Specifically with writing, it allows me to approach it fresh and clearheaded. The last thing you want when you're writing is the specter of *46 UNREAD EMAILS* looming over you. That doesn't lend itself well to existing in the moment.

Do you use an alarm to wake up?

Yes, but I'm not a big snooze-button guy. I wake up at a time that works for me and if it didn't I would change it. I also try not to pointlessly stay up late.

How soon after waking up do you have breakfast?

It depends on if I go out or cook with my wife. When we lived in New York, we would go out and work together most mornings at a restaurant. Sometimes I do that when I'm in Austin, but here we have chickens so we usually check the coop for eggs and cook something up. My office is right next to the kitchen so I am in and out of it anyway.

Do you have a morning workout routine?

I tend to work out in the afternoon. I'll run on the lake in Austin, or swim in Barton Springs. If it's a CrossFit day, I'll go to the early evening class. When I travel, my schedule is not as much in my control, so I go for a long run in the morning, then start the day knowing that however it turns out, at least I got a run in.

Do you also follow this routine on weekends?

Weekends to me are great examples of what life should be if we were better able to ignore distraction and obligations.

Saturdays and Sundays are productive and fun and relaxing. Why? Because there are fewer calls, and fewer demands on time. My fantasy is to someday get my Tuesdays to look like my Saturdays. Do what I want, stick to the routine I want, be indifferent to and insulated from all the noise. I try to treat Saturdays as a chance to catch up on stuff that I want to catch up on. I try not to let bullshit from the week creep in. I spend a considerable amount of time on the weekend working around my ranch. But it's fun work, the kind of work where I forget to check my phone for hours. It's also unpaid . . . or really, I'm paying to do it, but it's fun.

GEOFF COLVIN
Senior editor of *Fortune* magazine

When you shudder to imagine breakfasts
without your Japanese rice cooker.

What is your morning routine?

When I'm not traveling, I generally get up between 6:00 and
6:30 A.M. I drink three glasses of water, usually within sixty
seconds of getting up. It's amazingly effective at waking up
the body and the brain. I do a brief stretching routine, then
run five miles (six days a week). I'll then have breakfast,
shower, shave, dress, then get to work. Most of my work is
writing, which I do from home, so there's no commute.

How long have you stuck with this routine? What has changed?

I've been following this basic routine for ten or fifteen years.
The only changes have been minor tweaks to my insanely
regimented breakfasts.

What time do you go to sleep?

Generally between 9:00 and 9:30 P.M., so I get about nine
hours of sleep. That's a lot of sleep. I'm a huge advocate of
abundant sleep. Don't get me started.

Do you do anything before bed to make your morning easier?

I always read something having absolutely nothing to do with work, which makes going to sleep easier. Also, I don't drink. I was never a big drinker (two glasses of wine with dinner), but about eight years ago I realized that I felt better when I had no alcohol at all. I didn't quit in order to make my mornings easier, but it does make a difference.

How soon after waking up do you have breakfast?

Six days a week, breakfast is some combination of oats, plain nonfat milk, fresh fruit, dried fruit, walnuts, and some tea. On Sundays I make buckwheat-and-cornmeal pancakes, which I top with fresh fruit and plain nonfat Greek yogurt.

On my six-oat breakfast days I generally follow a rotation of four variations, all cooked with skim milk (not water): steel-cut oats, coarse ground oatmeal, rolled oats, and a combination of oat bran and Wheatena (a high-fiber, toasted-wheat cereal). Each of these variations cooks in the Japanese rice cooker while I'm running. I shudder to contemplate life without my Japanese rice cooker.

What are your most important tasks in the morning?

I'm a great believer in to-do lists, so every morning I make the list, then identify the most important items, and then force myself to do those first, which is usually hard.

What happens if you fail?

I just carry on, and if I miss the routine for only one day, it's no problem. Two days, and I feel a little sluggish. On the rare occasions when I've missed it for three consecutive days, I feel heavy, slow, and miserable.

Anything else you would like to add?

I would only emphasize that I love this routine. It's not self-denial. Obviously, it carries all kinds of health benefits, but I don't have to think about those. I love the feeling of running (especially outdoors), I absolutely love my breakfast, and I feel great all day long. I don't urge anyone to follow my particular routine, but I urge everyone to find a routine they love.

SHEENA BRADY

CEO of Tease Tea, merchant success lead at Shopify

When you're working two jobs at once and you're trying very, very hard not to multitask.

What is your morning routine?

I *try* to be up at 6:00 A.M. every day, as it takes about an hour until I'm mentally and physically ready to get to work. I run my company, Tease Tea, from 7:00 to 11:00, and lead my team at Shopify from 11:00 A.M. to 7:00 P.M. My morning usually looks something like:

6:00 A.M.—Wake up, let the dogs out, and make coffee. While the coffee is brewing, I stretch for a few minutes. I'll then brush my teeth, shower, and change, then meditate for ten to twenty minutes.

7:00 A.M.—Review my calendar for the day, schedule and time-block all actionables and tasks for the day. I'll then begin working, trying hard not to multitask and instead to stick to the time blocking.

9:30 A.M.—I commute to the Tease Tea office and fulfillment center. I chat with my sister, who works part time for the company. I ensure she has everything she needs to be successful for that day. I'll then meet with my digital marketing/community manager remotely, as well as our fulfillment/operations manager, who works out of the office. We talk about our goals for the day, roadblocks, and challenges, then we ask each other if there is anything we can do to support each other or remove any barriers to accomplishing anything.

10:30 A.M.—I wrap up whatever I haven't already accomplished on my to-do list. Usually it's emails by this point.

Multitasking versus Context Switching

When we describe multitasking we're often describing context switching, the act of opening up our email and looking through it for "just" two minutes before returning to our original task. Context switching is inherently bad for us—every time we switch between doing our work and reading an article online, or reading an article online and checking our phones, we experience a "transaction cost" that drains our energy and slows us down.

Multitasking is the act of doing two or more tasks at the same time, with varying levels of success. While most attempts at multitasking tend to fail (as anyone who has ever attempted to order groceries online while feigning an all-ears presence on a conference call will attest), certain activities can be worked in alongside each other, such as cycling to work (you get to where you're going while getting a workout in), or, if you can do it safely, listening to an audiobook in the car.

Whatever I don't finish by 11:00 I will pick up where I left off that evening, or the following morning.

11:00 A.M.—I start my day at Shopify. I'll see if there is anything urgent or pressing that requires my attention, then I'll go through my inbox and hash out any actionables. I lead a team of eight remotely from British Columbia to New Zealand, so they pop online at various times. I then attend any impactful meetings on my calendar for that day, including one-on-ones with each team member.

How long have you stuck with this routine? What has changed?

Almost a year now, though some areas can vary. I've learned to be realistic and give myself time in the morning, even if I work the first few hours at home. Giving myself that full hour to actually wake up in the morning and do what I personally want to do before any work has been incredibly impactful for my productivity.

GREGG CAREY

Entrepreneur, *Survivor* contestant

When weathering a cyclone on a desert island
makes you thankful for the basics.

What is your morning routine?

My morning routine is holistic and has four essential components. The details will vary, but the components are constant and critical to my happiness. They are:

- Energy: Eat something, drink something.

- Body: Work out (usually high intensity).

- Mind: Play piano, meditate.

- Soul: Connect to purpose, be grateful, feed cats, kiss wife.

Ideally, I wake up around 6:30 A.M. Special shout-out to Rufus, my cat, who is remarkable about waking me up at the same time daily. My routine can take anywhere from thirty minutes to two hours. My general goal is to always answer yes to the following question: If the day were to end after my routine, would it have been a successful and fulfilling day?

How long have you stuck with this routine? What has changed?

Adding piano was the biggest change. I've always loved music, but never played an instrument. I had assumed it would be the "one regret" that I'd take with me. Then, nearly two years ago, I began taking lessons from a jazz pianist.

The daily benefits piano provides me with are 1) meditation: you cannot learn without being completely present; and 2) skill development: every day I can say "I can do something that I couldn't do yesterday."

What time do you go to sleep?

Typically, I go to bed around 11:00 P.M. to midnight. Lately, I've been prioritizing my sleep in favor of my routine. I've realized that sleeping longer will always be the most beneficial thing I can do for myself. On those days, I will adjust my routine proportionally. I keep the components, but reduce the time.

Do you do anything before bed to make your morning easier?

I'll typically share a small cup of tea with my wife before bed. Her evening routine is as thoughtful as my morning routine, so I try to support her even though I can fall asleep anywhere at any time with absurd ease.

When I'm at my best, I'm evaluating the progress of my day and preparing in detail my goals for the upcoming day. When I'm at my all-time best, I'm implementing Benjamin Franklin's thirteen virtues.

Do you have a morning workout routine?

I'm a fan of high-intensity workouts. I've done stints at Cross-Fit, which I've loved. I've gone for long runs while training for a marathon. A ten-mile run in the summer followed by a cold shower is ten times as good as any cup of coffee.

What are your most important tasks in the morning?

Telling my wife that I love her. It's not a task, but it's important.

Do you also follow this routine on weekends?

I follow this routine on Saturdays, but usually take a day off on Sunday and let the day start and evolve more organically. I find it extremely important to go off script and switch off.

For me, the weekend always benefits from a strong Saturday morning routine. If I can put a good dent in my plan for the upcoming week, and have a good workout, then I feel much more free to truly enjoy the one-and-a-half weekend days ahead of me. A strong Saturday is key to a relaxed weekend, and it also helps to reduce any Sunday blues!

Benjamin Franklin's Thirteen Virtues

In a quest to achieve "moral perfection" as a young man, Benjamin Franklin made a list of thirteen virtues that he thought desirable, and attempted to train himself in each of them. (Franklin's biographer Walter Isaacson notes that the original list contained just twelve virtues. After seeing the list, a Quaker friend informed Franklin that he had left off something that Franklin was often guilty of: pride. Franklin added his thirteenth virtue, "humility," to the list, in a move consistent with the word itself.)

Primarily working on one virtue at a time, while always keeping the others in the back of his mind, Franklin kept a chart in which each virtue was listed alongside the days of the week. Every time he violated a virtue, he would place a dot in the appropriate place in his chart, with the goal of having placed as few marks as possible by the end of a week. Though Franklin is thought never to have recorded a clean sheet, the very act of attempting to do so was as beneficial to him in the late 1720s as it can be to you today. Franklin's thirteen virtues are:

1. Temperance: Eat not to dullness; drink not to elevation.

2. Silence: Speak not but what may benefit others or yourself; avoid trifling conversation.

3. Order: Let all your things have their places; let each part of your business have its time.

4. Resolution: Resolve to perform what you ought; perform without fail what you resolve.

5. Frugality: Make no expense but to do good to others or yourself; i.e., waste nothing.

6. Industry: Lose no time; be always employ'd in something useful; cut off all unnecessary actions.

7. Sincerity: Use no hurtful deceit; think innocently and justly, and, if you speak, speak accordingly.

8. Justice: Wrong none by doing injuries, or omitting the benefits that are your duty.

9. Moderation: Avoid extremes; forbear resenting injuries so much as you think they deserve.

10. Cleanliness: Tolerate no uncleanliness in body, cloaths or habitation.

11. Tranquillity: Be not disturbed at trifles, or at accidents common or unavoidable.

12. Chastity: Rarely use venery but for health or offspring, never to dullness, weakness, or the injury of your own or another's peace or reputation.

13. Humility: Imitate Jesus and Socrates.

You were on *Survivor: Palau*. Can you tell us about your morning routine on the island?

Survivor was a humbling experience that made me grateful for a lot we all take for granted. It was the real deal out there. I lost thirty pounds in thirty-three days. I weathered an overnight cyclone with barely any shelter. It makes you truly appreciate the bare necessities of life while recognizing we're capable of more than we think.

We began and ended our day with the sun. Each sunset or

sunrise would paint the sky in such a way that you couldn't help but quiet your mind and admire the beauty. This provided an opportunity to be grateful and find peace amidst the chaos. All strategy and "game play" would inevitably stop and we would appreciate life. And we'd just be so thankful for the basics: our family, our food, and our shelter.

MARIA KONNIKOVA

Writer for the *New Yorker*, author of *The Confidence Game*

When your day is so all over the place that your morning hours are your only chance for a little structure.

What is your morning routine?

I used to not be a morning person at all until I moved in with my husband almost ten years ago. I've since had to become one, as his work starts very early.

I normally get up around 6:00 A.M., and the first thing I do is make tea (because I need the caffeine), and then I have a morning yoga salutation practice to wake myself up. After that I'll have breakfast, shower, and then I'll get to the rest of the morning, which usually starts with checking email to make sure that there are no fires to put out before I start writing.

How long have you stuck with this routine? What has changed?

In the context of ten years, I recently upped the meditation component. I used to not meditate very seriously at all, and I still don't do it seriously compared to people who really do.

Meditation is a great way to organize your thoughts; I recommend it to anyone who wants to help bring themselves greater clarity and concentration. At the end of my yoga practice I'll sit for twenty to thirty minutes (more if I can afford it, but I usually can't) and really try to engage with the practice. I'll sometimes mix it up by going for a run afterward.

I'm someone who's generally not structured at all; my desk is a mess, my writing is a mess. When people ask me, "What's your approach to writing?" my answer is nearly always, "Throw up on the screen and see what happens," and that's really how I write. My brain is not an organized place, and the rest of my day is not at all organized either. The morning is my time to say "I got stuff done," and then I can go into the day thinking that at least I've taken care of something; at least I've had this little structure.

Do you do anything before bed to make your morning easier?

One thing I do, and it's hilarious that I'm bringing it up because I never follow it, is I have a planner and I write notes in it because I don't want my brain to have to actually remember that I have to do certain tasks the next day. I write everything down to get it out of my head, and then oftentimes I'll never look at it again.

How soon after waking up do you have breakfast?

I normally have breakfast a little over an hour after waking up. I always have the exact same thing, even when I'm traveling. I'm one of those people who, when you do radio interviews and they ask you what you had for breakfast, I always have the same answer: oatmeal with honey and blueberries.

Do you use any apps or products to enhance your morning routine?

No. I think some of these can be helpful for some people, but a lot of them, to be completely honest, are really bullshitty. We need fewer things to be stressed about in our lives, not more. I don't want to be worried that "Oh my god, I didn't get up correctly," because an app told me so.

What are your most important tasks in the morning?

I'm someone who's always working on multiple projects, and I'll often go from one to the other, so I try to figure out what I'm going to prioritize today, what I want to get done, and I try to kind of get into the mind-set for that. But I'm not very organized throughout the day, so I don't punish myself if, for instance, I wanted to get this done, but instead I got that done, because I realize you can't really predict how your mind is going to work on any given day, and you have to kind of embrace that.

Anything else you would like to add?

I don't think there's one perfect routine that's right for everyone. I think that everybody should find out what works for them. I hate when people write lists, like "These are the habits of creative people, and if you follow them you're going to be creative." It's interesting to know what other people do, but ultimately it's not a one-size-fits-all thing.

SHANE PARRISH

Founder of *Farnam Street*

When you take a stand against to-do apps and stick to basic,
old-school planning and discipline instead.

What is your morning routine?

Mornings are my most productive time of day. Over the
years, I've adapted my schedule accordingly so I can do my
most important work in the morning.

Energy levels and our ability to concentrate fluctuate
throughout the day. For most people, our ability to focus peaks
earlier in the day—prior to distractions, noise, and weakened
mental willpower. I dictate my morning routine before I go to
bed the night before. That's when I write down two to three
important projects that I want to concentrate on the next day.

I wake up around 6:00 to 6:30 A.M., grab a coffee, and
then sit down to work on those projects. I give myself sixty to
ninety minutes of uninterrupted time to focus on deep work*
and difficult problems. I then take a break, grab another coffee and breakfast, make note of any ideas that came to mind
that I want to revisit or research, and then work for another
sixty to ninety minutes on difficult problems or projects.

Do you answer email first thing in the morning?

No. This was a habit that I consciously had to break. If I got
up in the morning and the first thing I did was check email,

---

* The concept of "deep work" is described on page 65.

I'd be allowing others to dictate my priorities for the day. The important projects I want to focus on would get pushed back to later in the day, and I would be spending my most valuable mental-energy time answering emails that could easily wait for a few hours.

Do you do anything before bed to make your morning easier?

I write out my schedule for the next day. Scheduling keeps me on track and allows me to be conscious of how I spend my time.

How soon after waking up do you have breakfast?

My mind is typically awake before my stomach. Only after drinking coffee and completing a good chunk of work will I sit down to have breakfast. This usually consists of high protein and fat. I love bacon.

Do you use any apps or products to enhance your morning routine?

I'm not a fan of trying to solve common life problems with apps and software programs. Some basic, old-school planning and discipline do the job fine. And if you don't have discipline, an app won't help.

That's just my take. There's a certain amount of technology fetishism that creeps in. How the heck did Isaac Asimov write five hundred books without an app? He created a routine and stuck to it. Your habits become comfortable and customary.

What happens if you fail?

I try again tomorrow. Don't get into the habit of thinking it's all or nothing. Just get back on track immediately.

TODD HENRY

Author of *The Accidental Creative*

When you do your most creative work first thing,
and silence is your preferred soundtrack.

What is your morning routine?

On weekdays I wake up at 6:00 A.M. on the dot. I pour coffee (which I set to brew the night before) and then eat the same breakfast (oatmeal with frozen blueberries and a handful of cashews) every day in my home office while I study.

I spend the first hour of my morning studying and writing. I sit at my desk (or on the sofa in my office) and read a book with a pen in hand, taking notes and writing observations in my notebook for later review. At the close of the session, I spend fifteen to twenty minutes in silence—meditating or considering what I just read and how it applies to my life and work. Sometimes I also journal during this time.

How long have you stuck with this routine? What has changed?

Fourteen years. I used to try to cram everything into my morning routine, but I found that I do much better when I simply have an hour or so of study and thought first thing. It gets my brain moving, and it helps me get perspective on my day. Now, I have a list of "dailies" that I accomplish each day, but some of them I complete later in the morning or over lunch so that my morning doesn't feel so rushed.

Do you do anything before bed to make your morning easier?

I have a worksheet that I use to plan and execute my days. It has space to record my studying, my key tasks, and to track my dailies. It also has space for my daily "high," "low," and "learning." Each night I sit and plan the next day so I know exactly what I will do when I begin my work.

What are your most important tasks in the morning?

I write every morning. Every. Single. Morning. I am a firm believer in doing your most important creative work first thing.

What happens if you're traveling?

When I travel, my morning routine varies. I'm typically speaking at an event, so I do whatever I need to do to ensure the event is successful. That often means allowing my body some extra time to recover or taking a walk to get my blood pumping.

BILL McNABB

Chairman of the Vanguard Group

When you'll sacrifice everything to get enough sleep.

What is your morning routine?

I'm up between 5:00 and 5:15 A.M. I grab a coffee on the way to work and I'm at my desk between 5:45 and 6:15. Most days, I use this desk time to scan the news before responding to emails, particularly from colleagues in Europe and Asia. Meetings start at 8:00, and my schedule is pretty full for the rest of the morning.

How long have you stuck with this routine? What has changed?

My routine has varied about thirty minutes over thirty years. When I became Vanguard's CEO in 2008 (a position I held until early 2018), I started coming in a little earlier so I could have some additional preparation time in the morning. Other than that, not much has changed since I joined the company in 1986.

What time do you go to sleep?

Between 9:00 and 10:00 P.M. most nights.

Do you do anything before bed to make your morning easier?

I try to make sure I'm all caught up on email so I have a running start in the morning. I also read something non-work-related to relax my mind.

Do you have a morning workout routine?

Exercise is a key part of my daily schedule, and I try to fit in a midday workout three or four times a week. When meetings or travel make that difficult, I'll opt for a morning workout session instead. When I'm on the road, I always carry a TRX and a jump rope with me so I can exercise before the day begins. If there's a gym with full cardio equipment, I may jump on the rowing machine.

What are your most important tasks in the morning?

The quiet time between 6:00 and 7:30 A.M. is when some of my best work gets done. It's my time to read, think, and prepare for the day ahead. I try really hard to preserve that time.

What happens if you fail?

Quite simply, it stinks. If I fail to follow my morning routine it's usually due to lack of sleep. A late night means I'll often sleep in and go right to meetings in the office. That starts a domino effect, where my morning quiet time is bumped to lunch and my workout time gets bumped altogether.

The truth is, I'll sacrifice everything for the appropriate amount of sleep, even my morning routine.

MATTHEW WEATHERLEY-WHITE
Cofounder and managing director of the CAPROCK Group

When you realize you're way more productive when you're not in fight-or-flight mode.

What is your morning routine?

I'm fortunate enough in my life to wake without an alarm, so my mornings don't always start at the same time. If I could wave a magic wand to give everyone in the world one gift, it would be the ability to wake without that annoying, incessant beeping. There is nothing like simply opening one's eyes when they naturally want to open to make the world seem pretty much completely okay.

I'm *definitely* a morning person. Left to my own devices, I rarely sleep past 6:30 A.M., and I'm frequently up well before that. I wake quickly. Long, slow mornings are not part of my life; once I'm up, I'm engaged.

While I wait for water to boil, I usually run a mental preview of the day, check my calendar, and scan my email and texts to make sure nothing urgent has surfaced since I went to bed. Then I make tea or coffee, eat, and plug into a four-hour block of what I call "white space," from 8:00 A.M. to noon, which is blocked off on my calendar every workday and which only I have the authority to fill. Writing, business development, board meetings, exercise—whatever. It is how I bring a sense of intent and control to what is otherwise a primarily reactive work environment, and how I can structure a morning without imposing too much "structure."

Do you do anything before bed to make your morning easier?

The only thing I do before going to sleep (and not every night) is jot down a brief list of what needs to be accomplished at some point in the future. I frequently don't even look at the list when I wake up the next morning.

Do you have a morning workout routine?

My morning routine almost always involves exercise, and I'm an omnivore when it comes to activity. Running, riding some form of bicycle, skiing, yoga, rock climbing, resistance training, rowing, or surfing—just about anything will do, really, depending on the environment.

Exercise is my meditation, my grounding. I don't think of

it as "working out." Rather, I think of it as "working in," a way to bring calm, focus, and energy to all that awaits.

Do you use any apps or products to enhance your sleep or morning routine?

No. In fact, I do what I can to *reduce* the intrusion of technology into my morning. The last thing I want is to add more technology, even as I live with the benefits of technology elsewhere in my life.

What are your most important tasks in the morning?

Funny, I've never thought of it as a task, but the most important thing I do each morning is steady myself by not allowing a sense of urgency to penetrate. Every once in a while I find myself in a spin cycle of urgency—a sense of internal panic that the list of things to do is lengthening no matter how hard I try to control it. But I learned long ago (even though I occasionally forget!) that this sense of urgency is nearly always illusory. I am more productive when I am *not* operating with urgency.

I remember years ago reading a passage in a book about Thomas Keller in which the author marvels at the pervasive sense of calm in Keller's famous restaurant, the French Laundry. How could such incredible food, the author wondered, prepared at such exacting standards, be produced in such a calm environment? The irony is, of course, that the calm environment was the reason for the productivity, as it revealed total mastery of the task at hand. I strive for that same sense of calm mastery, and I occasionally even achieve it.

Stephen Covey's
Time Management Matrix

In *The 7 Habits of Highly Effective People*, Stephen Covey describes his time management matrix, which highlights, as Matthew puts it, the power of *not* operating with urgency.

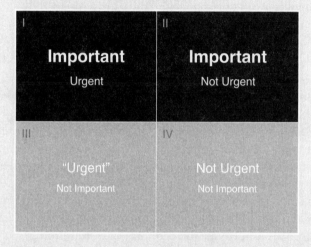

In Covey's own words: "The only way to make Quadrant I manageable is to give considerable attention to Quadrant II . . . [and] the only place to get time for Quadrant II in the beginning is from Quadrants III and IV. You can't ignore the urgent and important activities of Quadrant I, although it will shrink in size as you spend more time with prevention and preparation in Quadrant II." Thus, when you choose to *not* operate with urgency you can, over time, become more productive.

OVER TO YOU

"Whether the day is for writing, designing, or painting,
the consistent practice of a morning routine
is the doorway into it all."

—ELLE LUNA, ARTIST AND AUTHOR

Mornings are often when we're at our freshest, so it's no surprise that many successful people start their day by taking advantage of their first few morning hours to get as much focused and productive time in as possible.

This only gets more important with time. Illustrator and writer Mars Dorian notes that: "Over recent years my morning routine has become more tight and focused. The older I get, the less time I want to waste." Neuroscience PhD Darya Rose says: "Mornings prime your brain for how it will function the rest of the day. Are you going to be distracted and bounce around from project to project? Or are you going to be focused and choose your activities consciously and with intention? I much prefer to be in the latter state. I get more work done and it turns out better. I'm less stressed and less reactive. So I do what I can to keep my mornings simple and uncluttered."

Of course, this focused and productive time is not meant to come at the expense of your family, and it's important to find the right balance for you. Having a calm morning connecting with your family, whether they're at home with you or halfway around the world, will give you the fuel you need to work more effectively later in the day. In the words of the attorney general of Washington State, Bob Ferguson: "I like the kids to have a good start to the day. . . . It's easy for meetings to go late at work, or for other events to come up, and I'm not always guaranteed much time with them later in the day, so I like to lock in that morning time."

Start following the five points below, and see if your day starts to become more focused and productive:

WRITE A TO-DO LIST, THEN STICK TO IT

Having a to-do list and sticking to it is the number one thing you can do to increase your overall focus and productivity, period. We advocate writing out (whether on paper or digitally) your to-do list for the next day at the end of your workday (more on this in the Evening Routines chapter), so the moment you sit down to work you have it right in front of you.

You'll find your decision fatigue* is reduced, as you'll know exactly what you have to do that day, making it harder for you to jump around working on tasks that aren't important. Creating a to-do list liberates your mind from worrying about important tasks, as writing them down guarantees that you'll remember (and get to) them the next day. Judge Jeremy Fogel told us that every morning he "reflect[s] on what actually needs to be done (as opposed to the multitude of things that make demands on my time) and how best to accomplish that."

While we encourage this list to be aspirational and to represent a full day of work, don't overload the list and overwhelm yourself to the point that you feel paralyzed and, in

---

* Decision fatigue is described in detail on page 79.

turn, do nothing. We recommend keeping your list to approximately five to six items. Feel free to slip a couple of easy tasks in there to get some quick wins—the feeling of crossing out a completed task cannot be understated. If you find you can only complete three tasks per day, then lower your number. Even one major task on your to-do list is not too few.

When you think of new tasks throughout your workday, unless they're urgent and must be completed that minute—and there's a good chance that this will not be the case—add them to a separate list (or task "inbox," as it were). Then, when you go to write your next day's to-do list, you can move over some of the tasks that didn't get completed that day, as well as some tasks on your inbox list.

If you didn't write a to-do list the day before, that's okay. Write one in the morning just before you begin your work, but in general try to fit it in at the end of your workday so you can jump right into it the next morning.

DO YOUR MOST IMPORTANT WORK FIRST

Unless you're a shockingly disciplined person of your own accord, a to-do list isn't very helpful if you don't prioritize the items on it and, once prioritized, do your most important work first.

We've all been in a situation where we know the one or two tasks we should be working on, but instead choose to work on easier things. We like to refer to this as "positive procrastination," and while there's certainly some merit to it if it happens infrequently, for your to-do list to function correctly you must do your most important work first.

You already know what work this is for you. It may be unpleasant, but it can just as easily be highly enjoyable, something you desperately want to do but keep putting off, such as a personal project that benefits from your full attention.

In his 2016 book *Deep Work*, associate professor of computer science at Georgetown University Cal Newport describes "deep work" as: "Professional activities performed in a state of distraction-free concentration that push your cognitive capacities to their limit. Their efforts create new value, improve your skill, and are hard to replicate." This is counter to shallow work, described by Newport as "Noncognitively demanding, logistical-style tasks, often performed while distracted. These efforts tend to not create much new value and are easy to replicate."

This is your most important work. Or, to put it more succinctly, keep your mornings for thinking work, and your afternoons for minutiae.

DON'T CHECK YOUR EMAIL FIRST THING IN THE MORNING

For most of us, checking our email or social media accounts first thing in the morning spells disaster for our early morning productivity.

When you check your email first thing upon waking you're stressing your brain by jolting yourself awake to the realities of the day ahead. It makes you reactive instead of proactive, as you're jumping at the needs of others instead of addressing your own. As entrepreneur and author Julien Smith notes: "If I do email [first thing in the morning and] that's all I do, I hate my life."

Not checking email and social media makes it easier to stay in control of your thoughts. Remove push notifications and social media apps from your phone if you need the added discipline, or at least move these (and any other work apps) off the front screen of your phone, so you have to work harder to get to them. If all else fails, leave your phone in another room during the most productive part of your morning.

> "It turns out that the worst thing you can do with an email is answer it, because you get more back."
>
> —SCOTT ADAMS, CREATOR OF THE *DILBERT* COMIC STRIP

The moment you open your email you enter reactive mode, and you begin working on someone else's agenda rather than your own. This is true whether you're employed or self-employed. Do not let anyone (except your boss) get between you and your tasks for the day. The rest is just other people's problems.

Depending on how strict your workplace is, you can make modifications to this approach to ensure you're checking email less often in the morning while still not missing anything important as it comes in (and you never know, the longer you wait to reply to something, the greater chance the problem will resolve itself). In the words of software engineer and diversity advocate Tracy Chou: "I check email first thing in the morning, but I only respond to the ones where I can dash off one- or two-sentence replies." This is the perfect approach in this situation.

Be proactive in the morning, not reactive. You'll still be getting email when you're dead.

CUT OUT MORNING MEETINGS AND CALLS

If you find that your workday is frequently eaten up by meetings, try to get permission to sit out as many as you can. If you convince your boss of your willingness to work hard outside of these meetings, they'll likely allow it for the less crucial ones. (Make it a long-term goal to be able to sit out more and more.)

The potential to carry this out depends on your job, and indeed your level of seniority within it. With that said, we recommend trying to keep your morning meetings and calls to a minimum.

> "When I was running Paramount I had 8:30 A.M. breakfast meetings almost every single day. Two years after leaving Paramount, [I eliminated] daily breakfast meetings."
>
> —SHERRY LANSING, FIRST WOMAN TO HEAD A HOLLYWOOD MOVIE STUDIO

If your most productive hours are in the morning, it doesn't make sense to waste these on meetings and calls that, if we're totally honest, don't usually require you to bring your A game. Try to schedule meetings and calls for the afternoon instead. In the words of the author Laura Vanderkam: "When I'm scheduling my days well, I leave big open chunks of time in the morning so I can concentrate, and then I start phone calls after 10:30 A.M. I don't always stick to this, but I try."

If you're in a position where you can set boundaries on other people's requests, make it clear that your first available "slot" for meetings or calls each day is at midday before lunch, or from 1:00 to 2:00 P.M. after lunch. Then make sure these boundaries are respected (if you use a shared calendar, consider creating "unavailable" blocks for these morning hours), only giving exceptions, as the word suggests, in the most exceptional of circumstances.

BREAK DOWN BIG GOALS INTO SMALL PIECES

You've probably heard the expression "How do you eat an elephant? One bite at a time." While we personally advocate for a lighter breakfast, the expression rings true if you want to make the most of your morning to get your most important work done.

Nobody can dive headfirst into a big, scary project and expect to come out the other end having accomplished everything they set out to do. Work of this size needs to be reined in; it needs to be broken down into small pieces—or rather, eaten one bite at a time. If you want to get your most important work done in the morning, before the responsibilities of the day start to creep up on you, make sure this work is broken down into small, actionable pieces before you attempt to tackle them. These small pieces are far easier to get started on and work through to completion.

REVERSAL

The reversal here is clear. What if, despite your best efforts, mornings just aren't your most productive time of day?

In the words of author Chris Guillebeau: "The best routine is your own. I check email in the morning and don't exercise until later. If everyone else advocates the opposite, good for them. But you should always find what works for you, not for anyone else." In finding what works for you, be sure to go in with your eyes wide open and with the dedication to experiment with often polar opposite ways of working. Give everything you experiment with a week or two of your time before moving on to an opposing path, and equally giving this new path the time it deserves.

If you produce your best work later in the afternoon, or even well into the night, reverse the above points so you can deal with email, minutiae, and administrative tasks in the morning when you're least productive, leaving your most productive hours free for your most important work.

Do you have to check email first thing in the morning for your job? That's understandable, and we don't want to propose anything that would get you fired. In that case you can stick to a middle ground, choosing to filter your email inbox the moment you arrive at work so you can get a sense of what you'll have to deal with throughout the day, then immersing yourself in your most important work, dipping into your inbox every hour or so (or whatever feels appropriate) so you can still reply to any urgent or important messages as they come in.

As a coach and expert in workplace psychology Melody Wilding notes: "Most of us realize we're more productive at certain times of the day, but a key to benefiting from this information is being able to identify those times and adapt our schedule accordingly. Pay attention to the times when you're at peak productivity."

CHAPTER 3

MORNING WORKOUTS

Is Working Out in the Morning Right for You?

STEVE IS REALLY TAKING FITTING IN HIS
MORNING WORKOUT TO ANOTHER LEVEL

We all know we should exercise more, eat more health-ily, and spend less time in sedentary positions. Yet many of us struggle to find the time to fit a workout routine, however short, into our day.

You don't need to be spending two hours in the gym every morning to start to feel the benefits of a consistent exercise routine. In fact, keeping your routine short and easy to ac-complish will greatly increase the chances of you sticking to it, which will in turn help to ensure the long-term survival of your routine.

In this chapter we'll speak with (among others) retired U.S. Army general Stanley McChrystal about the differences between his workout routines in the United States and when he was deployed in Iraq and Afghanistan; Olympian Rebecca Soni on her love of running, swimming, and paddleboarding in the morning; and the CEO of Clif Bar & Company, Kevin Cleary, on why he's been tracking his weekly workouts for the past nineteen years.

GENERAL
STANLEY McCHRYSTAL
Retired U.S. Army four-star general

When you get up at 4:00 A.M. to work out because
the rest of your day's totally booked—and
miraculously, your body goes along with it.

What is your morning routine?

It varies, but I'll give you the general routine. I wake up about
4:00 A.M. and I get out of bed, shave, and then I work out for
about an hour and a half, and then I'll come back and spend
about four or five minutes taking a shower and cooling down
a little bit before heading into the office.

**How long have you stuck with this routine? What has
changed?**

I went through a period when I was just focused on running.
Every day I got up and I ran the same distance, seven days a
week. It was kind of crazy, and as I have gotten older I've
found that it's much better to alternate my workouts. One
day I run and then the next day I do weight training. I find
that by alternating the days of each activity I don't get injured as easily.

When I was deployed in Iraq and Afghanistan my morning routine was pretty much the same except I would often
break it into two parts. I would get up in the morning and I'd
do an hour run or something like that, and then at the end
of the day I would go back to the gym and I would do thirty-
four minutes on a cross trainer before going to bed. In Iraq

we worked all night, so we went to bed at about 6:00 A.M. just as it was getting light, and I slept until 10:00 A.M., and then I started my workout.

What time do you go to sleep?

This is going to be embarrassing. Probably between 8:30 and 9:00 P.M. My wife and I laugh about this; we've gotten into bed as early as 7:30.

Do you do anything before bed to make your morning easier?

I am a pretty organized person. I set my life up whereby I can get up in the morning and I can walk into the bathroom off our bedroom, and it's all set up with my running clothes; I've got a little shelf for my running shoes, and I have exactly what I know I'm going to need. So I can throw that stuff on and head out. I tend to always put things like that where they belong. If you make it hard to work out you won't do it. You have to follow the path of least resistance and make it easier to do it than not do it.

Do you use an alarm to wake up?

I use an alarm but I'm usually already awake and I'll just turn it off.

How soon after waking up do you have breakfast?

I don't feel good if I eat or drink anything before I work out. When I get back I'll have some water or some kind of ice drink. Once I get into work I'll drink coffee. But I typically don't eat anything until dinner. Now, every once in a while my body will say "eat something" at around midday, and I'll eat something, but most days I don't. It just makes me feel better, my body has gotten used to it, and so if I eat before dinner I get kind of sluggish.

Can you go into more detail about your workout routine?

I work out every day but I alternate whether I'm running or doing core. I don't take days off. With my running routine I get up, and I'll just run for over an hour. On the other days I do four sets of push-ups, and then I do this pretty strenuous core routine that will take me almost an hour. I also do a lot of ab exercises. I've had two back surgeries, and I've learned that the ab exercises help an awful lot.

After that I'll go to the gym and do upper-body stuff; wall, bench press, pull-ups, and things like that. If I get short on time, I find that if I get the abs stuff in and there's a little bit of yoga built into it, then I'll be good.

How does your partner fit into your morning?

My wife works out a lot, too. When I get back from my workout between 6:00 and 6:30 A.M., she will be getting up and heading out for a run. When she comes back from her run she'll go back out to go to the gym. We both have our own little routines that we don't violate.

Do you also follow this routine on weekends?

On the weekends my wife and I will both run at the same time, but we never run together. We run separate routes and then we'll meet at this little bagel coffee shop three blocks from our house.

My son, daughter-in-law, and two little granddaughters live next door to us, so we have this tradition where every Saturday and Sunday we all gather at the bagel shop (my wife and I will both meet there, and they'll trundle down with the kids).

What happens if you're traveling?

I travel an awful lot. Sometimes I'll get into my location at midnight, or even later. That affects me, but I tend to stick with my routine anyway. I just sleep less on those days, because I've found that as closely as I can stick to the basic things in my morning routine, the better it is for me. I've been doing a version of this routine for probably thirty-five to forty years.

In your book *Team of Teams* you reference "limfac," or limiting factor. What can be the limfac in your morning routine? And what do you do if you fail to follow it?

It's usually something I can't control, like I'll be out on the road and some client will want to do a 6:30 A.M. breakfast. What I've learned to do is get up at 3:30 and work out, and pay the price later.

I've learned that if I don't follow my morning routine, my mood is influenced, I look at the clock to see when I can work out; my body expects to do certain things at certain times, and I find if I don't do them I just don't feel physically right.

With your military background in mind, can you think of anything that our audience should try out in their morning routines?

You know, we tend to do what we like to do. When I first went to West Point I remember they made you do pull-ups, and I couldn't do as many as I was supposed to do. And so, now I do pull-ups every other day. It's like eating your spinach.

Find certain things you know you should do, don't like to do, or make excuses to avoid, and then do them every day or every other day, and then it just becomes a habit.

REBECCA SONI

Three-time U.S. Olympic gold medalist in swimming

When your morning treat is completely avoiding decision fatigue.

What is your morning routine?

I wake up around 5:30 A.M. and do a couple rounds of deep breathing to help me wake up. I'll drink a bunch of water, play with my cat and pup while getting dressed, and then go to the office to sit down for a ten-minute meditation.

I'll usually start the day with a workout. I run, swim, paddleboard, or do some yoga. It feels great to get everything moving before sitting down to work. This is followed quickly by breakfast and coffee. I try to eat breakfast (typically a bowl of oatmeal with a ton of fruit on top) before opening the phone or computer, instead of multitasking. But this is still more of a goal.

How long have you stuck with this routine? What has changed?

I've been doing this for a couple of years now. For the most part, I'll try to get in what I can from my list of morning routines for the day. From time to time this will shift, but in general it has stayed the same: Get up early. Center and balance. Go work out. Get to work.

Do you do anything before bed to make your morning easier?

I plan my day before going to bed. Being an entrepreneur working from home I have a lot of small decisions I need to make every day, so I've found this planning helps to avoid decision fatigue the following morning. If I have an early workout, I will prep my clothes the night before.

What Is Decision Fatigue?

Commonly recognized as a reduced ability to make decisions (or rather, to make the decisions you know you should make) due to being inundated with the sheer number of choices we're faced with on a daily basis, decision fatigue is a harmful psychological state that we all experience from time to time.

Examples of the effects of decision fatigue are all around us. A commonly cited example is that of judges handing down more lenient sentences, on the average, earlier in the morning compared to late in the afternoon. As John Tierney writes for the *New York Times*, describing a particular Israeli parole board: "Prisoners who appeared early in the morning received parole about 70 percent of the time, while those who appeared late in the day were paroled less than 10 percent of the time." Tierney goes on to note that to a fatigued judge, "denying parole seems like the easier call not only because it preserves the status quo and eliminates the risk of a parolee going on a crime spree but also because it leaves more options open: the judge retains the option of paroling the prisoner at a future date without sacrificing the option of keeping him securely in prison right now."

It's for this same reason that snacks and candy are almost universally found at the checkout line; grocery stores have wised up to the fact that after making dozens of small decisions over what brand of canned chili or breakfast cereal to buy, your willpower will be significantly reduced by the time you come to the checkout, and you'll be much more likely to throw a chocolate bar in your basket as you wait in line.

Typical methods for reducing decision fatigue in the morning include planning for the next day the night before, as Rebecca touches upon, and wearing a "uniform" to work every day (a tactic popularized by Steve Jobs, Mark Zuckerberg, and President Barack Obama). Long story short, the less unimportant decisions you have to make in the morning, the more energy you'll have for all the more important decisions you have to make later in the day.

What and when is your first drink in the morning?

Water, before my feet even hit the ground.

Do you also follow this routine on weekends?

Yes, though the workouts tend to be longer.

What happens if you fail?

I don't consider it failing, I just try to do the best I can every morning. I might end up feeling a bit more scattered throughout the day, but it motivates me to get it done tomorrow. Mornings are my favorite time of the day; I love the feeling of the possibilities of the day to come. It's great to have a routine that sets me off on the right foot.

SHERRY LANSING

Former president of 20th Century Fox and chairperson of Paramount Pictures, first woman to head a Hollywood movie studio

When your exercise routine is a second—
and equally important—job.

What is your morning routine?

Unless I have a very early morning, I wake up anywhere between 7:30 and 8:00 A.M. at the latest. I call my office right away, and I see to my email immediately. I address anything that wasn't completed the night before, or anything else on my to-do list, while I'm having breakfast. I get physical copies of the *New York Times, Los Angeles Times, Wall Street Journal,* and *Financial Times* every morning (my husband and I joke that because we can never decide who gets a particular section of a paper first, we should start getting two copies of each!), and I try to read them over breakfast before I work out.

Four times a week, I exercise. I do Pilates on Mondays and Wednesdays, and on Tuesdays and Thursdays I run on the treadmill for fifty minutes and do weights for forty minutes. I'd be lying if I told you that I never miss it, because I've missed it plenty of times. But I try very hard not to.

If I have an early morning meeting, which I have at least once or twice a week, I can't do the Pilates or the exercise. The part of my morning routine that I would most like to improve is making my exercise more of a priority and not constantly giving in when someone says, "Oh, the only time we can meet is 9:00 A.M.," and I say "Okay," and then I miss my exercise. I'm trying very hard to change that and make it the most important part of my day. It's about finding time for yourself.

How long have you stuck with this routine? What has changed?

For the past decade. When I was running Paramount I had 8:30 A.M. breakfast meetings almost every single day, so everything would be pushed a couple of hours earlier. I would get up between 6:00 and 6:30 A.M. and I'd exercise on the treadmill or exercise bike while either reading a script or returning phone calls to the East Coast (emails weren't as prevalent back then).

Nowadays I can read for pleasure much more—I never had any ability to do that before because I was so busy reading scripts all day.

What are your most important tasks in the morning?

Answering my email, reading the newspaper, and exercising. When I exercise in the morning, I feel great. I have to work on making this a priority. I always prioritize answering all my morning emails before I exercise, even nonurgent ones. I can't, with a clear conscience, exercise until all my work is done, until my desk is clear. I always put my duty before my exercise and I think that's a big mistake. I need to think of my exercise as a very important meeting.

What happens if you fail?

This all sounds very good, except you should know that I miss it a lot. I'm in a great mood right now because I haven't missed exercising for the last two weeks.

JILLIAN MICHAELS
Personal trainer, television personality

When your workout schedule is to squeeze one in
whenever you find a rare moment of freedom.

What is your morning routine?

My alarm clock is my five-year-old. He jolts me from slumber
at about 6:10 every morning for cuddles. Then we get up and
feed the animals (rabbit, pig, dogs, bird, chickens, ducks,
fish, etc.). Yes, I am serious.

I'll have coffee, and then we all make breakfast. After that
the kids get ready for school. Heidi, my partner, or I drop
them off, and after that the workday begins.

**How long have you stuck with this routine? What has
changed?**

For about three years now, since we've been living on a farm.
Because I have kids and many creatures to care for, my routine is pretty set in stone; they come first.

If I didn't have kids, I'm sure I would wake up, hit the
snooze button, have a quick five-minute meditation, and
then have coffee and catch up on the news for fifteen minutes.
After that I would probably start answering my emails while
having breakfast, and then I would shoot off to the gym. But
that is pretty much a fantasy for at least another thirteen
years.

Do you do anything before bed to make your morning easier?

I prep everything the day before. I make the kids' lunches so they are ready to grab and go. I prep all the animals' breakfasts. We lay out clothes for the kids.

Can you go into more detail about your workout routine?

I squeeze in my workouts whenever I can. I think it's so important to have portable, quick, and easy fitness solutions.

I created an app knowing that most people are strapped for time. They don't have the luxury of choosing when they train or of planning all their meals. My app allows you to work out anywhere, whenever is convenient for you, and it customizes the workouts based on your goals, time frame, fitness level, and the equipment you have available. Even the meal plans have simple, quick, easy recipes, and grab-and-go options to ensure you can be successful no matter how busy you are.

When do you check your phone?

As soon as I get out of bed. As a business owner, this simply comes with the territory. It's important to know if there is a problem brewing, and putting fires out early and quickly is a big component of success.

How does your partner fit into your morning?

My partner is exactly that—my partner. We divide and conquer the chores to get them all done.

What happens if you fail?

It really doesn't affect me. As long as I caffeinate and eat, I am pretty adaptable.

KEVIN CLEARY
CEO of Clif Bar & Company

When you plan your workouts around all
your other responsibilities.

What is your morning routine?

My day starts anytime between 6:00 and 6:30 A.M., and it always begins with exercise. I have three young boys—twins aged nine and the little guy is seven—and if I don't take advantage of the mornings, I don't know when I would find that time.

How long have you stuck with this routine? What has changed?

This routine has been on and off for probably about eight or nine years, but more intensely over the past four or five. I've been really focused on making sure I'm doing everything I can to make sure I'm in shape, especially as I'm an older dad.

The routine changes depending on what I'm doing at any given time. In 2016, I did Ironman Kona (a triathlon), so I really mixed in different types of exercises. A couple of years ago I was fortunate enough to get on the *American Ninja Warrior* show, and that tweaked the workout, but I try to stay pretty consistent about doing something physical every morning.

Do you do anything before bed to make your morning easier?

I get everything set up the night before. It just makes everything more streamlined. I lay out my bike stuff and my running stuff because I find that it gives me less to think about and more reasons to get up and go do it than delay. It's really where my wife and I are different. She's more spontaneous and I'm all into planning, but it works out well.

I make my protein shake in the morning, so I'll lay out all the pieces and parts for that the night before; I'll make sure I have water in the fridge, and I'll have my chia seeds and all that ready to go.

Do you use an alarm to wake up?

I use an alarm in the morning just for consistency's sake. Usually I'm up before it goes off. I can't remember the last time I hit the snooze button—I'll maybe hit it for a second and then my mind starts going like, "Let's get up, it's time to get going."

Can you go into more detail about your morning workout routine?

Every Sunday (I've been doing this for going on nineteen years now) I sit down and plan out my workouts for the following week—what I'm going to do based on my schedule, work, and kids. I always try to figure out what I'm going to be able to work on so I can manage my own expectations of what my workouts are going to look like for the coming week.

One or two times a week I ride my bike into work; it's about a forty-five-mile round trip.

What are your most important tasks in the morning?

When I first get to the office my most important task is to check in with my assistant to find out what we've got going on for the day. Is there anything that's emerging, is there anything new that we need to address during the day, or is the day pretty much going to go as scheduled, or at least as far as we can tell at that point?

That's really important to have; that connection with my assistant is a big deal. The other thing I usually do is check in with my wife to make sure that the kids have gotten off to school, and to make sure that the morning went well. Many times I'll get them breakfast in the morning when I'm not riding to work. And then I walk around the company and start to make sure that I'm connecting with people around the organization.

And if you fail to follow your routine?

I give myself a break and take the longer view of what's happening. If I can't do my workout later in the day, I'll tell myself I'll just pick it up tomorrow or the next day. Six months from now, my body and I won't know that I missed a day.

CAROLINE BURCKLE
U.S. Olympic bronze medalist in swimming

When swimming from a young age conditions your adult self
to wake up in the wee hours of the morning.

What is your morning routine?

I wake around 5:30 A.M., grab an energy bar, and hit the road
for my workout. This is typically a swim, a weight-training
workout, or a run-interval workout. Right now, I am in a six-
week "get fundamentally strong" block. This is what my week
looks like:

Mon: Swimming long, aerobic sets.

Tue: Slow strength training, focusing on isolating glute muscles, etc.

Wed: Running intervals (descending miles and/or tempo-
minute repeats), followed by a power-strength workout
that consists of power cleans, plyometrics, and/or banded
power exercises.

Thu: Swimming involving lots of arms, as my legs are dead at
this point (in essence, a recovery day).

Fri: Slow strength training (isolation) again and a short,
five-to-six-mile trail run (easy and steady).

Sat: Trail and/or flat running (long and smooth).

Sun: Stretching, rolling, etc. (off day).

How long have you stuck with this routine? What has changed?

I've had this routine my entire life! Swimming bred me to wake up in the wee hours of the morning from a young age. I try to have two days a week to "sleep in" to 6:30 or 7:00 A.M.

Do you use an alarm to wake up?

Yes (on weekdays), but typically my internal clock wakes me up about four minutes before my alarm anyway.

How soon after waking up do you have breakfast?

I eat a bar or some almond butter before I work out. After I work out, I have a three-egg scramble, half a grapefruit, and one of my delicious protein muffins.

Do you have a morning meditation routine?

Moving my body is my meditation. I typically find actual meditation to be more helpful for me during my midday break. I get going so quickly in the morning that I hit a wall right after lunch, and it is helpful to reset my mind and body with ten minutes of "me time."

How does your partner fit into your morning routine?

My boyfriend is absolutely phenomenal with this. He is an athlete himself, so it is a no-brainer for us to do our own things in the morning regarding workouts. And there is *more* accountability for us to push each other to sleep in and take recovery mornings.

What happens if you're traveling?

This is the hardest thing for a creature of habit, but I have learned to do *my* thing on the road, regardless. I pack accordingly and prepare things beforehand. Mimicking your environment as much as possible is so helpful, but adaptation is also crucial. Learning to adapt makes a better (and humbler) person and athlete!

And if you fail?

Over the past few months I have been working on truly letting this go. I have learned that it only affects me when I let it. Whatever I try to endlessly control ends up controlling me.

SARAH KATHLEEN PECK
Writer, long-distance swimmer

When you mentally say "ten to six" instead of 5:50 A.M.
to make your wake-up time seem less daunting.

What is your morning routine?

I have a couple of different morning routines depending on the day of the week and how the day is structured. Two or three times a week, I'm up and at the pool or off on a run.

The pattern is always pretty similar: I try my hardest to get to bed six to eight hours before I'm going to wake up, and then my alarm rings sometime between 5:50 and 6:50 A.M. (Mentally, I never say the word "five" about the time I'm waking up—it's always "ten to six," or "quarter to six.").

When the alarm goes off (this week, at 6:18 A.M.), I wake up, roll sideways to check my phone, then sit up and look out the window. I brush my teeth, go to the bathroom, grab a bit of avocado or half a banana, and fill up my water bottle. I try to drink a lot of water before I get to the pool, usually around

6:50 A.M. We swim a 3,000- to 3,500-yard set, and it's all over by 8:15.

At least twice a week, however, I let myself sleep in. During the winter months I can hibernate like a champ. Sometimes I'll go to bed around 11:00 P.M. and stay there until 8:20.

Sundays are my "delicious" days. So long as I'm not traveling or doing some big event or race, I stay in bed as long as I want. When I have those Sundays off, I like to watch the sun come up, listen to the traffic outside, and pad to the kitchen in my slippers to get a cup of coffee. I'll then sit in my bed and read whatever strikes my fancy, sometimes an *Economist* issue cover to cover; other times I catch up on all the urban patterns and prints I like to study, and sometimes I just graze across all my friend's tweets and postings and read some of my favorite blogs.

How long have you stuck with this routine? What has changed?

This has been my routine for the past couple of years. In college, I woke up at 5:29 A.M. four times a week for morning practice, and on the weekends I was at the pool by 8:00. I feel positively indulgent in my routine today, although it's still fairly similar—just not quite as rigorous.

What time do you go to sleep?

This is a rhythm, too. Probably twice a week I stay up because I find my stride after work hours and get lost in a writing piece that I'm working on. This happens to me a lot on Friday nights. I don't go out that much (or at least I try not to), and in my college years I developed the habit of "Fridays in, Saturdays out" because we always had 8:00 A.M. practice on

Saturday mornings. I love the idea that Friday has an extra five hours of time that you can create if you want to use it.

How soon after waking up do you have breakfast?

I have a hard time digesting bread products in the morning—cereal has never done it for me. I like to eat something with a lot of fat or protein in it. My favorite breakfast is avocado, kale, and eggs. I feel like Popeye with his spinach when I get my Superman breakfast.

If I'm running late—or off on a morning workout—I have a stack of protein bars, which are wheat-free, low sugar, and have some good protein in them. I basically look for foods that burn slowly so they keep me satiated for longer.

Can you go into more detail about your morning workout routine?

My workouts tend to be part of larger "sets" or structural rhythms. I tend to focus on an event each season as my workout target. During the summer I'll do some open-water swimming and training; sometimes I'll train for a half marathon or a run; other seasons I'll focus on dancing. I like to think of my workout goals as three to four months out, and then I vary it by season. It's probably the high school athlete in me—I'm so used to a fall, spring, and summer sport that I still live by it.

What do you do if you fail to follow your routine?

It can be disorienting, but I've gotten fairly good at adapting to it. I've traveled enough and had enough experiences when I don't get the right amount of sleep, or something comes up, and that's life. It's always a little different and it's far less predictable than we'd hope.

OVER TO YOU

"I go to the gym on Mondays, Wednesdays, and Fridays. My goal is to simply go and spend fifteen minutes there. Building the habit is more important to me than sticking to a particular routine."

—DAVID KADAVY, AUTHOR AND PODCAST HOST

Working out is akin to doing a good deed for your body and making an investment in your future health. Not only does working out have positive physical effects, it should also be valued as a meditative exercise that can help bring comfort and clarity to your day every morning. As Yolanda Conyers, chief diversity officer at Lenovo, notes, working out is "as much about mental clarity as the physical benefits."

Working out in the morning brings these physical and mental benefits to you first thing upon waking; and as with any element that you want to add to your day, doing it first thing in the morning provides you with the triggers to make sure it will actually happen. Numerous studies have concluded that though there are some differences between morning and evening workouts—working out before breakfast means your body will burn a greater percentage of fat instead of carbs, whereas working out in the evening may have the upper hand for pure strength training—the key to sticking to a workout routine is to do it when it feels best and is most convenient for you.

> "Three times per week I visit a gym for a full hour of foam rolling, stretching, cardio, weights, and general agony."
>
> —DES TRAYNOR, COFOUNDER OF INTERCOM

Here are some hard-earned tips and suggestions on how to embrace a morning workout routine:

VARY YOUR WORKOUTS

Keep your workouts fluid, both on a day-to-day basis to keep things interesting, and throughout your life as your needs change. James P. Owen, a forty-year veteran of Wall Street and the author of *Just Move!*, told us: "As I get older, I've found that day of recovery has become more important. But I'm not one to sit around for long, so I do thirty minutes of walking outside, just to get the blood flowing, and thirty minutes of stretching later on in the day."

Similarly, General Stanley McChrystal noted: "As I have gotten older I've found that it's much better to alternate my workouts. One day I run and then the next day I do weight training. I find that by alternating the days of each activity I don't get injured as easily."

Though you should alternate what part of your body you work out from one day to the next, to build in time for muscle recovery and to ensure that you stick to your workout routine and don't fall off the bandwagon, you should also do it to stave off boredom. While it's good to create a morning workout routine, the motions themselves don't have to become stale and monotonous.

MAKE YOUR WORKOUTS SHORT AND SIMPLE

This is especially important in the beginning, when you're testing the waters of a new routine element. Vice president of product design at Facebook, Julie Zhuo, told us that she likes to do just ten to fifteen minutes on her elliptical first thing in the morning, instead of having the whole back-and-forth of going to a gym. "I try to keep it low pressure," she said. "This way it's like brushing your teeth. It's not a big event."

You're just looking to oil the chain, to get the blood pumping, to warm up your body, and to make it possible for you to perform at your best throughout the day. There's nothing wrong with push-ups, squats, jumping jacks, or just standing up beside your bed and getting in some stretches. Remember: Done is better than perfect.

Start by incorporating the simplest of these exercises into activities you're already doing in the morning, maybe flowing through yoga poses while your morning coffee is brewing, or doing jumping jacks while waiting to get into the bathroom.

> "I do light yoga stretching before I do my push-ups. . . . Nothing too extravagant, just mainly concentrating on my breath and one good yoga flow—at least five simple minutes to gather my thoughts while getting a good stretch."
>
> —MORGAN JALDON, MARATHON RUNNER

Former U.S. Navy SEAL Brandon Webb told us that he always fits in fifty push-ups and crunches alongside yoga stretches every morning as a short exercise separate from his gym workout later in the day. This, he said, is in case he can't get to the pool, a gym, or a yoga class while out on the road.

EMBRACE THE EARLY MORNING SWEAT AND THE FEELING OF ACCOMPLISHMENT IT BRINGS

For many of us, if we don't get to our workout in the morning, it won't happen later in the day, however good our intentions. Once the pace of the day speeds up, leaving what we're doing to work out can seem both impractical and irresponsible.

> "Starting my day with exercise gives me a big mood and energy boost throughout the day and makes me feel like I've accomplished something right off the bat. One of the big keys for me is getting dressed in running clothes right when I wake up, because it sets the default to exercise—my family expects it, and I expect it too."
>
> —JAKE KNAPP, AUTHOR AND DESIGNER

When you embrace the early morning sweat, you know that regardless of anything else that happens (or doesn't happen) throughout your day, you got your workout in. You can then take this "win" into the rest of your day. As UX designer and product strategist Sarah Doody puts it: "I can always look back to my morning workout and think, "I ran ten miles this morning, so I can handle _____."

RUNNING MAY BE YOUR GATEWAY DRUG

Maybe you've never been a runner, or maybe you've given it a chance in the past and concluded that it's not for you. That's okay, and we're not going to try to convince you otherwise (but these folks might).

"Exercise is an essential part of my morning. I go on a walk or run through the Marin hillside every day with my dogs. This is an aspect of my routine that I cannot sacrifice since it helps me feel centered and ready to take on any challenges the day may throw my way."

—KARA GOLDIN, FOUNDER OF HINT WATER

Running can be your gateway drug into a healthier lifestyle and can even give you the momentum to design a whole new morning routine. Strategic coach Arvell Craig notes: "Running helped me become the morning person I always wanted to be," while the writer Paul Schiernecker says: "A year ago I managed to completely kick smoking and have been running [ever] since. Then, I couldn't run a mile. Now I do between three and five."

We recommend you run through a park or another green space if you can, and avoid city streets and treadmills. The fresh air really will do you good, though the most important factor is that you're out there running, however you go about it.

DON'T MAKE IT AN OPTION NOT TO

The easiest way to stick to your new workout routine is to make not sticking to it not an option. Laying out your workout clothes the night before and keeping everything you need packed and ready to go is the classic guardrail. We'll touch upon this more in the Evening Routines chapter.

Consider forming an accountability group (or partnership) to help encourage you to work out when you say you're going to. Simon Enever, cofounder of a toothbrush start-up, does this well: "Team sports are good because you can't let the team down by not turning up. Unlike a solo activity like going to the gym or for a run, a team sport forces you to go (and you always end up enjoying it)." In a similar vein, you may find that your partner can be the person to push you to stay accountable to yourself.

Financial Ties

Accountability groups are one thing—the social ties and sense of honor that force you to follow through on a promise cannot be undervalued. In a similar vein to accountability groups, expensive gym memberships are the classic example of a financial tie that encourages you to do what you said you were going to do by making it financially painful not to. Even better are classes that make you pay a deposit to save your spot, or the often-cited example of giving a not-insignificant sum of cash to a friend and telling them to donate the money to a cause you would never want to give money to or have your name associated with (your least favorite politicians are often a good choice) if you don't follow through with what you said you would do.

If all else fails, consider working with a personal trainer. Although not cheap, this could be the best investment in your body you ever make. A trainer will keep you honest and push you hard.

REWARD YOURSELF

This reward can come during the workout itself (particularly if you work out at a gym) or later in the day.

If your motivation needs an immediate boost, give yourself the reward of watching an awful television show while you're at the gym. It's the only time any self-respecting adult can get away with this, so pick wisely! If you work out outside, then being out in the great outdoors is reward in itself, but don't feel that you can't still give yourself something later on.

REVERSAL

Unless you're suffering from a physical injury or health condition, we can't in good conscience let you off the hook for working out.

The reversal here is in the timing of your workout. While the majority of successful people do work out (78 percent of everyone we've interviewed when this book went to print), the timing of their workout routines vary, with many instead choosing to work out in the afternoon or early evening. As Bill McNabb notes: "Exercise is a key part of my daily schedule, and I try to fit in a midday workout three or four times a week."

Working out in the afternoon is a great way to give you more energy for the workload ahead, and it can reenergize you to get through the rest of your workday. (It can also serve as a marker of the end of your day, if you prefer to work out in the evenings.) If the morning is your most productive time for creative work, then pushing your workout routine to the afternoon or early evening is absolutely fine, and indeed encouraged. As the journalist Ann Friedman told us: "Morning is my most productive mental time; exercising in the morning feels like a waste of my best writing hours."

CHAPTER 4

MORNING MEDITATION

Can Meditating in the Morning
Help You Focus Throughout the Day?

I'M SO JEALOUS OF JOHN, HE'S REALLY
GOT NOTHING GOING ON UPSTAIRS

Meditation can take many forms, and some of the examples you're about to read are on the advanced end of the meditation practice spectrum. But please don't dismiss this chapter for that reason alone. Even if the idea of sitting down to meditate for twenty minutes every morning doesn't appeal to you, you can learn to find meditative moments in the mundane and generally build in moments of mindfulness throughout your day for greater energy, focus, and calm.

Meditation can include everything from heaving yourself into the lotus position (often against your best judgment) at a weekend retreat, to waiting patiently while your teakettle boils, to playing with your kids in the morning. Here are some of the most common types of meditation:

- **Guided:** Nowadays, the typical guided meditation involves an app or audio program talking you through your practice. Another option is going to a meditation class or retreat where someone in the room leads you (or a group) through a succession of mental prompts.

- **Mindfulness:** In this discipline, it's just you and your breath. When you imagine meditation, this style is likely what you're thinking of. When your mind starts to wander during mindfulness meditation, gently bring it back and return to focusing on your breath.

- **Zen (Zazen):** Unique to Zen Buddhism, zazen is a form of meditation typically performed in the lotus position (or simply with your legs crossed). Posture is important, and it's not uncommon for Zen Buddhist priests to sit zazen for more than twelve hours at retreats.

- **Transcendental:** Also called TM, this is a form of silent mantra meditation whereby you close your eyes and repeat a mantra in your mind for fifteen to twenty minutes in a row, twice a day.

The list goes on to include Vipassanā, Mettā, qigong, self-hypnosis, prayer, and more modern ideas on what meditation can include, such as journaling, running, and walking in nature. If you come at this habit with a genuine curiosity and openness to new experiences—without taking it too seriously (at least in the beginning)—you'll crack open a whole new mental frequency.

> "On days I don't have time to do anything else, I just pray and meditate, as I find those to be the most important components of a good start to my day."
>
> —LISA NICOLE BELL, ENTREPRENEUR

In this chapter we'll speak with (among others) the president of Pixar and Walt Disney Animation Studios, Ed Catmull, on why he chooses to focus on his breath in the morning (he hasn't missed a day in years); author, filmmaker, and Zen Buddhist priest Ruth Ozeki, on her sixteen-hour meditation retreat sessions; and writer and meditation teacher Susan Piver, on how she works to make her mind remain dreamy in the morning.

RUTH OZEKI
Novelist, filmmaker, Zen Buddhist priest

When your morning routine depends on
the role you're playing that day.

What is your morning routine?

I love the idea of a single, perfect, infallible morning routine,
and I'm always searching for it, but unfortunately I have yet
to find it. Meanwhile, I have several routines, which I'm always changing and which vary depending on where I am,
who I am, and what I'm doing.

So, for example, during the school year, when I'm being a
professor and going to school and teaching classes, I usually
wake up at about 7:00 A.M., brush my teeth, wash my face, sit
zazen, make coffee, and then I try to get a couple of hours of
writing in, at which point I turn my attention to schoolwork,
planning classes, reading student work, meeting with students, and teaching.

When I'm being a novelist, living on a remote Canadian
island in Desolation Sound, I wake up around 8:00 to 9:00,
brush my teeth, wash my face, sit zazen, and then write more
or less for the rest of the day. Sometimes my husband, Oliver,
brings me coffee in bed, in which case I noodle around, writing in my journal first, and watching the deer nibbling the
heads off the yellow flowers outside the bedroom window,
before I move on to zazen and fiction writing.

When I'm being a Zen priest at a meditation retreat, I
wake up at 4:30 A.M., brush my teeth, wash my face, and then

sit zazen from 5:00 A.M. until 9:00 P.M., and then go to bed. (Sometimes I sneak a little writing in, too.)

How long have you stuck with this routine? What has changed?

I started teaching at Smith College two years ago, so that professor routine is still newish and I'm still working out the bugs, but the other routines I've had for quite a while now.

I'm always observing and tweaking my routines. I am a big believer in the Hawthorne effect, which was first identified in 1958 and describes two very interesting sociological phenomena: 1) That research subjects (in this case factory workers at an electric factory) were motivated to improve their performance simply because they were the subjects of a study and their behavior was being observed, and 2) that when a change was made to one of the variables in their working conditions (in this case, the levels of light at the factory workstations), the novelty led to temporary increases in productivity—in other words, the determining factor was the fact of a change, rather than the specific change itself.

The Hawthorne effect suggests that 1) the novelty value of change in a routine can lead to increased productivity, but 2) the productivity increase is temporary, so 3) it's good to change things up from time to time.

I treat my life as an observation experiment in which I'm both the experimenter and the subject. I establish a routine, change a variable, and observe my performance, and when the novelty wears off, I tweak the variable again. If nothing else, it keeps things interesting.

Do you do anything before bed to make your morning easier?

Sometimes before I go to bed I'll think of a problem I'm trying to solve in the novel or piece of writing I'm working on, and then in the morning I'll lie in bed and think about it, and often I'll find I've come up with an idea or solution during the night.

Do you use an alarm to wake up?

If I have to wake up at a certain time, I use my phone alarm, and I try very hard not to snooze. But sometimes if I'm woken during a particularly interesting dream, I'll snooze in order to go back and finish it. Of course, this rarely works, but it's fun to try.

Can you teach us more about your morning meditation routine?

I practice zazen. I like to meditate first thing in the morning, except on those mornings when Oliver brings me coffee in bed. I find it's easiest to sit before getting caught up in the busyness of the day. I like to sit for half an hour. Sometimes, when I have a lot to do, I'll only sit for fifteen or twenty minutes, but even ten minutes is better than no minutes. And sometimes I do zazen at night instead of, or in addition to, the morning. Night zazen is nice, too. It has a different feeling, quiet, dark, and settled.

What and when is your first drink in the morning?

Coffee. I used to drink Sencha (Japanese green tea), but switched to coffee a few years ago. Oliver came back from Los Angeles with a Japanese ceramic filter, and insisted that it was better than either a French press or a Melitta. I thought he was being ridiculous, but then we did a blind taste test, and he was absolutely right. He had a long explanation as to why—something involving the physical properties of the pointy design of the conical filter and the shape of the spirals on the interior of the filter holder, but I've forgotten the details. He hand grinds the beans in an antique German burr grinder that we bought on the street in Berlin. It's just a wooden box with a crank on top and a little drawer to collect the ground coffee. The coffee is excellent and always tastes better when he grinds it.

How does your partner fit into your morning?

Often we make each other coffee, and sometimes we have breakfast together. Back when Oliver and I first started living together, he liked to listen to the radio first thing in the morning, but I don't. When I'm writing, I like to go from the dream state of sleep to zazen and then directly to the page. It takes me a few hours before I can safely let in the world, so Oliver now just reads the news.

What happens if you're traveling?

I'm never really settled in a single physical home, so I'm constantly adapting my routine to fit whatever environment I'm in—sometimes Massachusetts, sometimes New York City, sometimes British Columbia, and oftentimes on the road in hotels in different parts of the world. But zazen helps with this. It's the single constant factor, wherever I go. If I can sit down to meditate, then I feel like I'm home.

And if you fail?

I just pick myself up and try again the next day. As long as you keep on getting out of bed, you never really fail, right?

Anything else you would like to add?

I said at the beginning of this interview that I was looking for a single, perfect, infallible routine, but after answering these questions, I see now that not only is this impossible, but I don't really want it after all. I enjoy the different roles I play in my life, and I enjoy the routines that they require. I enjoy observing all my routines and constantly tweaking them. Change keeps my routines fresh and my mornings interesting. I like it that way.

ED CATMULL

President of Pixar and Walt Disney Animation Studios

When you have to tackle the internal discourse
in your head before you can relax.

What is your morning routine?

I wake up, go downstairs, and start making a cup of coffee. I use three shots of espresso, mix in three tablespoons of cocoa powder (not Dutch process), and two sweeteners. I've heard this helps you think better; I have no idea if this is true, but it tastes good.

I drink the coffee while I first check email, then read the news: the *New York Times,* the *Wall Street Journal,* and the *San Francisco Chronicle.* I then check one of the news aggregators, which I didn't use to do, but the train wreck of public discourse nowadays is too hard to ignore.

How long have you stuck with this routine? What has changed?

I have been doing this for many, many years. The only changes are that my schedule is busier now, so it interferes more with my morning workout schedule.

Do you use an alarm to wake up?

I set the alarm for around 5:45 to 6:15 A.M. I use a progressive alarm that makes a soft sound at first, and then progressively gets louder. But I usually wake on the first sound, so it doesn't disturb my wife. When I used a loud alarm clock, I was more likely to hit it on the head and go back to sleep.

How soon after waking up do you have breakfast?

I usually have a smoothie or some cereal for breakfast. My smoothie is typically some kind of plant protein powder (I am intolerant to milk protein) in almond milk, some frozen berries, and a dollop of almond butter.

Do you have a morning workout routine?

I exercise in the gym about three times a week. I vary the workout every time but I'll always do some type of circuit work with weights. It gets my heart rate up without putting too much stress on my knees, which for some reason seem to be older than the rest of my body.

Since I live in San Francisco, there are plenty of hills. I like to walk down and then run up, landing on the balls of my feet since it is easier on the knees. I eagerly await the day when there is a replacement for the meniscus (the piece of cartilage that provides a cushion between your thighbone and shinbone). It is such a beautiful and simple-looking disk;

you would think by now that medical scientists would have a material to match it. Ideally, I would prefer to have this before I need a knee replacement, or die.

How about morning meditation?

I meditate every day (I haven't missed a day in years) for thirty to sixty minutes before working out. It is always some form of Vipassanā meditation, such as focusing on the breath. I have received a great deal of benefit from the simple yet difficult practice of learning to stop the internal voice in my head. I learned that that voice isn't me, and I don't need to keep rethinking events of the past, nor overthink plans for the future. This skill has helped me both to focus and to pause before responding to unexpected events.

I will admit, however, that even though I am focusing on the breath, an idea will sometimes just pop up that's worth keeping. If I hang onto it, it messes up my meditation. So I just jot it down and let it go. There is something a little catchy to this phrase.

What happens if you fail?

I never miss my meditation, although I may shorten the time if I have to leave early. If I don't exercise, I start to feel crummy, but I'm pretty good about holding myself to my schedule.

AISTE GAZDAR

Founder of Wild Food Cafe in London's Covent Garden

When you spend your morning ironing things out in your mind
before the hustle and bustle of the day begins.

What is your morning routine?

I get up between 4:00 and 6:00 A.M., usually around 5:00. I
use an alarm clock as a backup but I usually get up just before the alarm rings. The moments before fully getting up
and jumping out of bed are really important to me. I say to
myself "I am awake," and that goes to all levels of my being,
not just the physical, but the mental, emotional, and spiritual
as well. I stretch my body from head to toe, take a deep
breath, and get out of bed.

In the bathroom I use cold water to make sure that all my
senses are fully awake and in tune. Then I start my exercise
routine with something called Mayan yoga, an ancient style
of native South American exercises designed to consciously
stretch, move, and stimulate the heart and mind, to make
sure that the energy within us moves harmoniously. It is a
combination of gentle stretches and some vigorous movement, followed by a relaxation. Afterward, I do a series of sun
salutations, finishing with a short meditation and prayer.

If I'm not in a rush to leave, I'll use the time until 8:00 or
9:00 in the morning to study anything unrelated to business.
Subjects that really interest me, but which I would otherwise
never find the time to learn. I use this time to learn to play
instruments, read nonfiction books, study astrology, or go
for a walk in nature.

How long have you stuck with this routine? What has changed?

It took a long time for me to gather the courage, discipline, and commitment to follow this routine, but I find it to be a game changer.

I used to struggle to get up in the mornings, mostly because my mind associated rising early with duty, school, obligation, conveyer-belt careers, and all the things that didn't excite me in the slightest. I purposely engineered my life so that I didn't have any obligation to get up early, and I loved it, until I got a strong message to change a few months ago. Waking up early in the morning sends a very important message to myself and, without sounding too wacko, to the universe: "Hey, here I am, awake, aware, sharp, and ready with the first morning light." I find that being conscious and awake early in the morning gives enormous power, strength, clarity, vitality, centered awareness, and focus that the evening just cannot provide.

Giving myself time, care, and attention in the morning has been crucial to significantly reducing my stress levels and consistently increasing my capacity to perform, have clarity, and take action.

Do you have a morning meditation routine?

My morning meditation is probably the most important aspect of each day. I see it as "making your bed" for the day. Whatever external or internal struggles I might have, meditation is the opportunity to iron things out from the other side of conscious awareness without any thinking or doing—just by becoming super aware of the vastness, depth, and richness of my being. Once I'm in that state, everything falls into place, even if I don't yet know what those things are.

DARYA ROSE

Neuroscience PhD, author of *Foodist*

When you realize that checking email before you meditate
is like downing a double espresso before you go to bed.

What is your morning routine?

I'm very fortunate to have a home office, so I don't have a
commute.

I wake up without an alarm on most days, often with the
sunrise. I usually have coffee and hot muesli with cinnamon
and unsweetened hemp milk for breakfast. If possible I like
to meditate for thirty minutes after breakfast, before checking email. I never check email before breakfast. Email is one
of those things that can easily seep into your life and add
stress to everything. The key realization for me was that
there's no point in opening email unless I can actually do
something about it in the moment (for example, it is hard to
send important documents from my phone, so I wait until
I'm at my computer). When I see emails that I can't take care
of, my mind starts thinking about them, and I can't let go of
them until I take action. I knew this intuitively, but it became
incredibly obvious to me when I started meditating.

When you meditate you try to focus on one simple thing,
like your breath. When other thoughts come in you just ac-
knowledge them and let them go. I noticed that if I had
checked email before meditating it was far harder to focus
on my breath, with most of my intruding thoughts coming
from obligations that I had seen in my inbox. I've since found

that it's much better to get focused and centered first, then tackle email later.

How long have you stuck with this routine? What has changed?

I've stuck with the meditation part for four or five months. Meditation has had a huge impact on my ability to concentrate and on my general well-being. I feel less frazzled.

Mornings are important as they prime your brain for how it will function for the rest of the day. Are you going to be distracted and bounce around from project to project? Or are you going to be focused and choose your activities consciously and with intention? I much prefer to be in the latter state. I get more work done and it turns out better. I'm less stressed and less reactive. So I do what I can to keep my mornings simple and uncluttered. I have coffee, eat breakfast, and meditate before doing anything else.

Do you use any apps or products to enhance your morning routine?

No. I like to keep my mornings old-fashioned. I carefully construct the habits and routines in my life. One reason for this is that the strength of habits is that they let you do important things automatically, without much thought or willpower. To this end, the less you are dependent on extraneous products and apps, the more likely you are to succeed in creating a strong habit.

MICHAEL ACTON SMITH

CEO of Calm

When you start your day with a group meditation
and end it with a bedtime fairy tale.

What is your morning routine?

I wake up at 7:30 A.M. and usually potter about for a bit in a
daze trying to remember who I am and what day of the week
it is. If it's a nonfoggy San Francisco morning, I'll make a cup
of tea and sit in my living room to watch the sun come up
over the bay. I'll usually drink a glass of water and then, if I'm
feeling energetic, I'll go to the gym.

After the gym I'll shower, get dressed while listening to a
news briefing, then walk to work via a coffee shop. I'll spend
about an hour in the coffee shop making calls to the UK,
writing to-do lists, reading the news, and answering messages. I'm a big fan of working from coffee shops in the
morning as I believe it's valuable to have a space between
home and the office. It's gives you a chance to plan and think
about the day ahead before being thrown into the noise and
interruptions of office life. I love getting into a flow state
when working, and coffee shops seem to be the perfect environment for me to achieve this.

**How long have you stuck with this routine? What has
changed?**

About a year and a half—ever since I moved to San Francisco. It's a lot simpler and more organized than it used to be
in London. Back then I had a tricky commute from Soho to

Shoreditch, which made it difficult to plan much of my morning other than trying to stay sane on the Central line.

Do you do anything before bed to make your morning easier?

I put my phone into airplane mode, then plug it in to charge, face down, on the floor by the bed. I'll read before bed most nights as I find it a great way to relax and unwind. Ninety-five percent of the time I read nonfiction.

Do you have a morning meditation routine?

Unsurprisingly, I use Calm! We start every day at Calm HQ with a group meditation. We do the Daily Calm together (a ten-minute meditation on a different subject every day). It sounds unusual and very "California" but it really is a great way to start the day with the people you work with.

In the evenings, if I'm stressed at the end of the day and my mind is racing, I'll take a bath with Olverum oil. On weekends I'll usually start the day with a meditation at home in my living room, or occasionally I'll go to Golden Gate Park and meditate in the sunshine. Learning to meditate has definitely improved my sleep by making it easier to switch off when thoughts start swirling around and taking over. At Calm we recently launched Sleep Stories, which are bedtime tales for grown-ups. They are a simple but very effective way to help people relax and drift off.

Do you answer email first thing in the morning?

Unless there's an emergency or we're in the midst of a big launch, I try not to open my phone until I've left the house and am sitting in a coffee shop.

Most people open up social media and email before they've

even got out of bed, but I find that's a rough way to start the day. I think it's important to let the mind keep wandering and daydreaming first thing in the morning before it gets sucked into the dopamine-frazzled craziness of the online world. I usually have my most creative ideas while I'm in the shower or getting ready for work, but if I have just read something sad or negative online, my mind will be racing away in a very different and less productive direction!

What happens if you fail?

I don't worry about it. Mornings are important because they set us up for the day, but if we're too strict and regimented we take the fun out of them, and life can become pretty dull. As with most things in life, it's a balance that we should be constantly playing with and tweaking.

SUSAN PIVER

Author of *Start Here Now*, meditation teacher

When you try to keep your mornings soft and quiet
so your mind can remain dreamy.

What is your morning routine?

I get up between 4:30 and 5:30 A.M. I used to attend solely to what I would call the foreground: thoughts, actions, and habits. However, the Buddhist view, as I have been taught it, is to focus equally on what is relegated to the background: underlying motivations, the physical space I inhabit, feelings and moods, and the moment's textural quality.

To do this, I try to keep my mornings soft and quiet so my mind can remain dreamy for as long as possible. Before I get out of bed, I think of my teachers. I rouse an image of their faces or a sense of their presence. I thank them and experience the goodness of my relationship to them. I request their companionship, whatever that might mean. Then I get up, put on my robe, and walk outside to my office, which is in the apartment across the courtyard from where we live. I don't say hello to my husband, pet the cat, or stop for anything. (Since it's so early, no one has to see me out and about in my jammies.) I turn on the kettle and make a huge mug of Irish breakfast tea that I get from a tea shop on Sullivan Street in New York City. Only that tea. Period. While it's steeping, I take a very short, cold shower and then "open" my shrine by lighting a candle and making a tea offering to my lineage (which simply means putting a small cup of tea on the altar). I make sure my workspace is basically tidy. Then I sit down on the couch to write in my journal, which results in some meandering and blathering followed by the daily writing out of three instructions, which are:

1. Take no shortcuts. (In work, love, and especially when it comes to my meditation practice, which is not a life hack or a self-improvement device.)

2. Shame is the enemy. (When it rears its puny head, remember gentleness, I tell myself.)

3. Protect and nourish your body. (Think about what I'm going to eat and when I'm going to move.)

Finally, I write down something that one of my idols said to me about my work. It's way too flattering and nice and I would be very embarrassed to share it here, but I like to remind myself that he said this. Every day. It makes me feel so happy.

Then I practice sitting meditation for a period, followed by a particular Vajrayana Buddhist liturgy I have been working with for fifteen years. After this, on really good days, I write something. Anything. Five hundred words. At this point, the routine ends. It's maybe 9:00 A.M. I manage to do this entire routine about 60 percent of the time. I'd really like to up that to 80 percent.

And then I really never know what to do next. Sometimes I eat breakfast, sometimes I don't. Sometimes I exercise, sometimes I don't. It's infuriating. I have tried to become more routinized by reading books, hiring experts, consulting oracles, and setting my alarm clock ever earlier. But linear methods pie me in the face every time. Over the years, I've learned that instead of pushing myself to create something, it is more useful to see what I can allow to arise. My commitment is to remain seated and wait. This is how it works best for me.

I have a lot of sadness. This has turned out to be fruitful in its own strange way. Sadness is actually a very soft, open, and workable state. I find that when I stay with it, I have easier access to what qualifies as success for me: greater wisdom, insight, meaning, creativity, and love. These qualities all have one thing in common. They arise from the space just beyond conventional thought. One cannot command them. So sadness is a sort of gateway to success beyond Susan, which is my true aim.

How long have you stuck with this routine? What has changed?

Over a decade. My morning routine changes by degrees with the seasons of New England. I sleep less in the warmer months and spend more time outside. I also feel less sad. Or sad about different things.

Do you have a morning meditation routine?

I am a Buddhist teacher with an online meditation community. Our core practice is Shamatha-Vipashyana or mindfulness-awareness practice. I make guided instructional videos every week for nearly twenty thousand people. Each video is preceded by a short talk. This is my work. So much of my day revolves around meditation. (This is not necessarily a good thing, by the way.)

How does your partner fit into your morning?

My husband is so kind to me about my morning routine. This has taken some adjustment because he is the sort of person who enjoys life more when we are together, and I enjoy life more when I am alone. Over the past twenty years we've grown to accommodate each other thanks to his big heart. For my birthday last year, he bought me a painting of a small house in a big, open field. Over the canvas, the artist wrote, "Leave me alone, leave me alone, leave me alone" dozens of times. It meant so much to me that he recognized my nature even though it is antithetical to his. That was really romantic.

What happens if you fail?

I try not to beat myself up, and find something delightful about falling through the cracks. I remember the words of the Tibetan meditation master Chögyam Trungpa Rinpoche: "The bad news is you're falling through the air, nothing to hold on to, no parachute. The good news is there's no ground." If I can remember this, I relax.

OVER TO YOU

"Meditation is the greatest life hack
that most people don't use."

—RAVI RAMAN, EXECUTIVE CAREER COACH

While this chapter is not designed to be an expansive study of the benefits of meditation or the different practices of meditation available to us, we will take some time to look at some simple ways in which you can work a mindfulness practice into your morning routine, no matter how busy you may be.

If you've never meditated in your life, please don't skip over this section. Here we're going to show you that meditation can take many forms, and that to dismiss it because you're picturing the over-the-top legs crossed on a mountain peak version of meditation is a mistake. Meditation has found a resurgence in popularity in recent years for an unsurprising reason: it can have a profound positive impact on your life, especially if you stick to it over the long term. Meditation can help improve your concentration, helping you to see clearly when looking at a problem; it can help bring you out of a rut, opening your eyes to the world that you always knew was there, but had somehow forgotten; and it can help reduce stress and improve your sleep. In the words of news correspondent and meditation advocate Dan Harris, meditation "won't fix everything in your life, [it won't] make you taller, or (most likely) land you in a state of bliss on a park bench. But it can make you 10 percent happier, or maybe much more."

Maria Konnikova adds: "Meditation is a great way to organize your thoughts. I recommend it for anyone who wants to help bring themselves clarity and concentration." While David Moore says: "Meditation is easily my favorite part of the morning because I'm deliberately setting the tone for what I'd like to accomplish."

Meditation takes many forms, and it's up to you to find what type of meditation works best for you. We're not talking about the relative benefits of Transcendental Meditation versus zazen, or Vipassanā versus Mettā, but rather that of simply practicing mindfulness (the act of clearing your thoughts and focusing on the present) on your daily commute or during your morning run or, if you can find the time, for five to ten minutes of sit-down practice. As Darya Rose put it in her routine: "Meditation has had a huge impact on my ability to concentrate and on my well-being in general. I feel less frazzled." This section is designed to show you just how easy it can be to bring mindfulness into your morning routine, if only you'll allow it.

Here's to feeling less frazzled.

FIND MEDITATIVE MOMENTS IN THE MUNDANE

If you're not yet ready to call a full meditation practice your own, start looking for meditative moments during otherwise mundane events.

"I hand grind tea leaves and wait while they steep. This is the closest thing to meditation that I do. The manual process of clipping, crushing, and steeping the leaves wakes up all of my senses."

—VANESSA VAN EDWARDS, BEHAVIORAL INVESTIGATOR

You can find a meditative practice in making breakfast every morning, or while grinding your coffee beans or steeping your tea. Former aerospace engineer Amit Sonawane told us that for him: "Meditating is an act of simply being aware. I tend to do that when I am making a fresh pot of coffee (the smell, the feel of cold water as I wash the pot, the gentle warm steam on my face as I bring the cup closer for a sip)." If you wanted to turn this into a full meditation practice later on, you could use one of these mundane processes to help time your practice. Computer programmer Manuel Loigeret notes: "While the water is boiling, I sit and meditate for ten minutes." If you have a timer set for one of these tasks already, all the better.

MEDITATE ON YOUR MORNING RUN OR COMMUTE

It's been said that running is something of a moving meditation, and this appears to be backed up time and again when we speak with people about it. Over the years of interviewing hundreds of people for our website we've found that we consistently speak with people who consider their morning run or commute to work on public transportation a form of meditation. Facebook product designer Daniel Eden told us that: "People gripe or wonder about [my] commute, but I like the forced headspace it can foster."

Morning workouts of all kinds can be meditative, but there's something about running in the morning that seems to lend itself particularly well to meditative thoughts. And though commuting to work on public transportation may sound like the least calming practice in the world, there's a lot to be said for sticking on a pair of headphones and, whether you let a prerecorded meditation guide you or you just listen to something to block out the noise, letting yourself escape the world around you for just a little bit.

CHOOSE WHAT COMES AFTER YOUR MEDITATION PRACTICE WISELY

You'll recall that one of the pillars of being able to form a new morning routine is being able to use each element (or habit) within your routine as a trigger for the element that comes after it.

If you choose to create your own morning meditation practice, you will be wise to follow it with something that can benefit from any insights you picked up during your meditation. Yoga teacher and cofounder of Bad Yogi, Erin Motz, notes: "I meditate for ten minutes and then immediately put pen to paper and write . . . It's usually stream-of-consciousness stuff or my thoughts about any random topic I think of." Similarly, singer-songwriter Sonia Rao told us: "I meditate for thirty minutes each morning and free-write for another thirty minutes. I'm not sure what type of meditation this is, but I just sit up against my headboard on my bed and focus on my breath."

BUILD IN MOMENTS OF MINDFULNESS THROUGHOUT YOUR DAY

Whether you build a designated morning meditation practice for yourself or not, be sure to scatter small spells of mindfulness throughout the rest of your morning, and your day generally, to help you stay present and focused.

> "Journaling is my meditation. Writing in my notebook clears my mind and helps me stay rooted in gratitude. Without my daily journaling practice, I'd be less grateful and full of joy."
>
> —TAMMY STROBEL, AUTHOR AND PHOTOGRAPHER

To everyone who's more aware of small spells of irritation throughout the day, here's what Melody Wilding had to say: "There are so many benefits to mindfulness, so I make a point to search for reflective time throughout my day, even if it's in small ways. If I'm stuck on a long line or delayed on the subway, rather than be annoyed, I see it as an opportunity to reflect and practice being present and in the now."

DON'T TAKE YOUR PRACTICE TOO SERIOUSLY

A disciplined practice will build with time if you want it to, but for now don't allow any performance anxiety to creep into your meditation practice. Yoga teacher Gracy Obuchowicz notes: "I've studied a few kinds of meditation but none of them too seriously. Mostly, I just sit and notice and feel. I do alternate nostril breathing. My mind wanders and I bring it back. My practice isn't fancy but [it] seems to do the trick of keeping me centered."

Don't feel that your meditation practice should be one type or another, or that you have to stick to someone else's rules. You know better than anyone what is calming and meditative for you.

REVERSAL

There is no reversal to finding meditative moments throughout your day. While you may not have the time or inclination to build a meditation practice into your mornings, it is beneficial to build moments of mindfulness and reflection into other parts of your day. Engineer Andrew Caldwell puts this perfectly: "When the river is calm and the sun's coming up, taking a bit of time out to be quiet and breathe properly . . . that might count for something."

CHAPTER 5

EVENING ROUTINES

Your Morning Routine Starts
the Night Before

CLARK, IS THERE SOMETHING YOU
WANT TO TELL ME?

Most people spend their evenings running up the hours before they're finally bored enough to go to bed. Sometimes a social event is to blame, or a pressing work deadline, but most of the time we avoid going to bed because we know our main block of leisure time is about to come to an end.

The solution isn't to beat yourself up, but to structure an evening routine that helps you wind down from the responsibilities of the day and get a head start on your morning.

In this chapter we'll speak with (among others) the founder and president of Bob's Red Mill, Bob Moore, on why reading historical biographies before bed sometimes helps, yet sometimes hinders, his sleep; math educator José Luis Vilson on the importance of calming your mind in the evening; and author and speaker Jenny Blake on why watching TV late into the night is never worth the trade-off of sacrificing her morning routine . . .

DAVID KADAVY

Author of *The Heart to Start*, podcast host

When your evening routine helps your brain
work better in the morning.

What is your morning routine?

I'm not a morning person, which is exactly why first thing in
the morning is my most critical creative time. Research shows
that your off-peak times are the best for insightful thinking,
so my one goal in the morning is to make the most of that
still slightly groggy time.

I wake up without an alarm, usually around 8:00 A.M. Ideally, I'll meditate for about ten minutes, but I'm usually too
eager to start working. I set up my computer on a bookshelf
that allows me to stand while working, put in some earplugs,
and spend the first hour of my day on my most important
project. Usually, this hour turns into around two hours of
uninterrupted work.

How long have you stuck with this routine? What has changed?

I've guarded my first hour religiously for the last six months,
but I've made it a priority to work first thing in the morning
for about three years.

I used to have the goal of working just ten minutes straight
on a project first thing in the morning. I'm always shooting
for a goal that feels ridiculously easy to me as a way to trick
me into working more. I've gotten better at focusing, so just
one hour is a pretty easy goal for me.

Do you do anything before bed to make your morning easier?

The more I wind down the night before, the better my brain works in the morning. On a perfect night, I'll have turned off all screens or put on blue-blocker goggles by around 10:00 P.M. I also try not to read any social media or things that make me think about anyone other than close friends and family after this time. (The exception to this is long-form stuff, such as books.)

I may watch a show or some videos, but I try to spend the time after 11:00 doing only quieter activities, such as reading. I go to bed before I'm too exhausted, and I like to sit in bed with the light on and stare at the wall when I first get in. I allow myself to think about the things that happened that day or what I'll do tomorrow, and only when my eyelids start to get heavy do I put on my sleeping mask, insert my earplugs, and turn out the light. I've found that if I try to close my eyes before my eyelids get heavy, I have a hard time sleeping.

Do you have a morning meditation routine?

I try to meditate for ten minutes each morning (sometimes I'll extend it to half an hour). I first concentrate on my breath, and then I search my body for points of tension that I allow myself to release.

Do you also follow this routine on weekends?

On weekdays, my first priority is to do some work. On weekends, my first priority is to get outside for a short time. I plan my coming week on Sunday afternoons and often have to spend time organizing my life and travels on Saturdays as well. I generally don't work on weekends unless I'm really crunching a project.

JENNY BLAKE
Author of *Pivot*, speaker

When your evening routine begins at 3:00 in the afternoon.

What is your morning routine?

Ideally, if I have gotten at least seven to nine hours of sleep, I get up before the sun rises (5:00 to 6:00 A.M. is a dream), but sometimes I get up closer to 7:00 or 8:00. I love reading nonfiction books, with a candle lit, for an hour or two until the sun rises. Afterward, I meditate for anywhere from twenty to forty-five minutes before starting the day. Every now and then I'll go for a twenty-minute run to get some fresh air and my endorphins pumping, but usually I save my workouts for later in the day.

How long have you stuck with this routine? What has changed?

I have been doing a variation of this routine for as long as I have worked for myself after leaving Google six years ago.

I realized very quickly that my body—and by extension, my routines—were the fuel for my business. If I was operating at 50 percent effectiveness due to lack of sleep or exercise, then as its sole employee, so would my business. That was unacceptable to me! Not to mention unsustainable. Success, to me, has as much to do with how I run my business and my life as it does what I choose to work on. I came to adopt the motto "Your body is your business," and I make my physical health and vitality a top priority. My staples are yoga, meditation, Pilates, walking, eating well, and getting plenty of sleep. Those elements of my happiness formula are what lead me to be my energetic and creative best.

What time do you go to sleep?

If left to my own devices, I love going to bed as early as 8:30 P.M., which most of my friends make fun of me for. I'm the opposite of a vampire. If I go out to an event or dinner with friends, I'm usually asleep by 10:00 or 11:00. I look forward to quiet mornings so much, before the rest of the world is awake, that I really prioritize what time I go to sleep. I don't have FOMO (fear of missing out) for nighttime parties, I have it for the glorious mornings I might miss out on if I stay up too late.

Do you do anything before bed to make your morning easier?

I start to wind down for the evening as soon as I leave the house in the afternoon for yoga or a walk with a friend. That means I don't respond to email (unless I feel like it or there's something particularly pressing), and I don't put pressure on myself to check it at all after 5:00 P.M. I'll have dinner around 6:00 or 7:00, watch a show, read a little bit, then go to sleep.

As I lay my head down on the pillow, I love the nights where I remember to go through my set of "wind-down" questions. They allow me to clear my mind, and often help me fall right asleep. Here they are: What was my highlight of the day? My low? What is one thing I'm proud of or want to celebrate? What is one (or more) things I'm grateful for? What is one unanswered question I'm facing?

Do you use an alarm to wake up?

I don't use an alarm unless I have a flight to catch. I also don't schedule meetings or coaching calls until at least 10:00 (preferably 11:00), which helps me avoid a feeling of rushing out of bed to start the day. I figure that my body will rest as long as it needs to.

Do you have a morning workout routine?

Working out is my reward later in the day. I work very diligently and focused from 10:00 A.M. to about 3:00 P.M., then I head out for a walk, a yoga class, or a Pilates class. I often meet up with a friend for coffee or dinner as a combo with one of those activities, or afterward. My favorite way to catch up with people is "walk and talks," which makes the conversation more engaging and has the added benefit of exercise.

How about morning meditation?

Meditation is my medicine! It is the best thing I can do for my day, and it helps me feel calm, grateful, grounded, strategic, and creative. I usually do a minimum of twenty minutes. I don't practice any particular style, rather I vary it from day to day.

I have steadily increased the amount of time I give meditation over the years. It used to be ten to twenty minutes a day (sometimes just five), until I realized that it was actually *the* most important thing I could do in a day, not something to be squeezed in. It dissolves problems much more quickly than churning through them all day with my mind.

Do you answer email first thing in the morning?

One of my worst habits used to be reading email from my pillow first thing upon waking up. What a horrible way to start the day! I felt stressed and annoyed before even getting out of bed. Now I try not to bring my phone near my nightstand, and I don't check email until I have accomplished one to two hours of work on my most important projects for the day.

NIR EYAL

Behavioral designer, author of *Hooked*

When you use technology enthusiastically all day long,
then cut off your internet connection at night.

What is your morning routine?

I use a lot of technology throughout my day, and I use a lot of products that help me quantify things that are important to me. Sleep is one of the things that is very important to me.

I use a smart timer every morning that wakes me up around 7:00 A.M. It comes with a little device I attach to my pillow that communicates over Bluetooth to a little receiving station. When it detects that I'm stirring at around 7:00, it wakes me up within thirty minutes of that time, so sometimes I get up around 6:30, sometimes a little later.

I get up, greet my wife, go to the bathroom, then perform a quick phone check. I'll then make my coffee and sit down with my family before I go ahead and start writing.

How long have you stuck with this routine? What has changed?

I've always woken up at around 7:00 for as long as I can remember. I'm constantly tweaking my morning routine. Something I'm currently experimenting with is skipping breakfast.

I started that about four months ago to see how it affects my day-to-day routine.

What time do you go to sleep?

I'm in bed by 10:00 P.M. My internet shuts off around that same time; I have a router that specifically shuts off the internet connection to many of my devices, and then I'm sleeping by around 11:00.

Do you do anything before bed to make your morning easier?

I like to have a clean desk, I think that's something that helps me right after I make my coffee in the morning and sit down with my family. If I have anything on my desk, there's a good chance it will provide a distraction for me, so I clear it all away.

What are your most important tasks in the morning?

My most important task is to properly greet my daughter and wife. We're big fans of the habit of showing appreciation to each other throughout the day, so we have a routine of every morning giving each other a big hug, kiss, and saying good morning and that we love each other.

What happens if you fail?

I have a few things that I check off every day that are important for me to do. At my desk I have a big whiteboard right in front of me that has my routines, and they include two hours of writing five days a week, going to the gym four days a week, taking a walk with my wife two days a week, and then reading twenty pages in the book I'm currently reading five days a week.

All these things I do throughout my day, not just in the morning, and I have a little check mark that I put next to each of those things so I can see if I've done it. If something comes up, I'll try to reschedule that activity for some time later in the week, to make sure I get everything I need to get done in that space of time.

JOSÉ LUIS VILSON

Math educator, author of *This Is Not a Test*

When you hit up Jay-Z and Daft Punk in the morning,
and a cup of chamomile tea at night.

What is your morning routine?

I wake up at 5:30 A.M. I drink a cup of water, eat my cereal, get dressed, and run out the door to work. Sometimes I'll take a bus to the train, and sometimes I'll walk, depending on how much time I have. On the train, I listen to mood music. If I'm in a good mood, I'll listen to some Jay-Z or Daft Punk, but if I'm in a funky mood, I might try some Kendrick Lamar or Radiohead. If I'm somewhere in between, I'll bump the Hamilton soundtrack.

After I get out of the subway, I grab a small cup of coffee and get my mind ready to teach. I start thinking about the students in my class, what periods I have to teach, and what activity I'll be doing that day. I find myself changing my energy depending on the first and last classes I have, and whether I'm giving a test or quiz. To do this I might shake myself out or stretch. I'll take some deep breaths as I would in meditation.

How long have you stuck with this routine? What has changed?

I've done a similar routine for the better part of a decade. In some ways it's gotten better, and in some ways it's gotten worse. When I lived farther from school I'd have more time to read books and grade work on the subway. On the other hand, because I now live closer to work, I can get to work much earlier and spend time getting ready for the students.

What time do you go to sleep?

Around 10:30 P.M. If I go to bed any later, I know tomorrow is not going to be a good day.

Do you do anything before bed to make your morning easier?

I usually drink a cup of chamomile tea to help me sleep better. I put the water on to boil and put some honey in it to sweeten it up a bit. This calms me down and keeps me hydrated throughout the night. I also try to let go of whatever happened that day. It's not good to sleep with anger, rage, or any extra emotions.

Do you use an alarm to wake up?

I use an alarm to wake me up, but on most days my body wakes me up about seven minutes before it sounds. I leave my alarm in the kitchen. It's usually loud enough for me to hear, so I have to get up and keep myself upright so I don't go back to sleep. I don't hit the snooze button if it's a school day.

Do you have a morning workout routine?

No. Though because it's New York City, I get in about three thousand steps before I even get to work.

Do you also follow this routine on weekends?

On weekends I don't have to teach. I might sleep a little longer and take my time eating breakfast. I'll also watch the news or *Sesame Street* with my son, and respond to emails more carefully. I don't necessarily sleep in on weekends per se, but I steal a couple of hours where I can.

BOB MOORE

Founder and president of Bob's Red Mill

When you wear a lot of hats, literally and figuratively.

What is your morning routine?

I have a pretty steady wake-up time of 6:00 every morning. I can't seem to sleep in much on Saturdays and Sundays, so I'm usually up around the same time on weekends.

I have a very interesting life. I'm president of Bob's Red Mill Natural Foods. We have about five hundred people here in Milwaukie, Oregon, three shifts, 24-7, so it's a busy place making whole grains and shipping them around the world. It's always fascinating for me to come down here early in the morning or late at night and walk the plant and say hello to people. That's what my life is all about.

How long have you stuck with this routine? What has changed?

I've been in business most of my life. I opened my first garage and service station when I was twenty-five. I've always been an early riser; this current 6:00 A.M. wake-up time has been my wake-up time for probably the last twenty-five to thirty years. If you're going to go into business for yourself and you're going to hire people, the first thing you have to do is set an example to your employees. You can't just laze around.

What time do you go to sleep?

I don't go to sleep quite as early as I should. I've had a tendency to burn the candle at both ends all my life, and there are times when I get worn down, so I try to be out of it by 10:00 P.M. If I'm asleep by 9:30 or 9:45, I feel very happy, as that gives me eight hours of sleep.

Do you do anything before bed to make your morning easier?

I have a lot to do before I go to bed. I need to shower, I need to lay my clothes out for the next day. I like to read.

I'm into biographies and history, and I like to allocate a certain amount of time each day to reading things that I'm interested in. Right now my fascination is with Churchill, and I have a delightful book written by his youngest daughter, Mary Soames, who wrote an autobiography that includes her father and her activities with him, especially during the Second World War when they were so active over there with the Axis powers. So, I'll get started reading something like that and it will just draw me in and it'll be hard for me to go to sleep at night. I very often wake up at 10:30 or 11:00 P.M. and realize that I've fallen asleep reading.

With that said, reading a book often keeps me awake rather than helping me fall asleep, which is interesting. There's always a book beside my bed and I can't wait to keep reading it every night, especially this one by Mary Soames. I've actually awakened at least twice this past week at 2:00 or so in the morning and read for a while because I'm just so fascinated by it. I'm old enough to remember the Second World War and a lot of the activities, and she is touching such interesting memories and nerves for me that it's hard to set it down.

How soon after waking up do you have breakfast?

I'm not someone who jumps out of bed and has to have breakfast right away, but when I do I'll typically have one of my whole-grain cereals. If I believe anything in the world, it's that a whole-grain, hot, cooked cereal is the best thing to start the day with, and I do believe it is an element of a long and healthy life. I have proven that to myself and I feel very strongly about it. I feel slighted when I get up in the morning and circumstances like traveling make it more difficult to get what I want for breakfast.

Do you have a morning workout routine?

I walk a lot. Here at the plant we have seven acres, and we walk a lot. Well, we certainly talk about walking a lot. . . . To be honest I wouldn't want to hang anything expensive on my walking on a regular basis.

When do you check your phone?

I'm always checking it. I use my phone to write out whole long conversations I've got so comfortable typing on it. I never send a message that has a typo, ever. I read them over and make sure they're just right before sending them. I make sure that every one of my communications is grammatically correct before sending.

What are your most important tasks in the morning?

I wonder what shoes to wear, as even though I lay all my clothes out the night before, I still need to know what shoes, coat, and hat to wear. I always wear a hat, I have about a hundred hats, and I have duplicate pairs of shoes in black and brown, and my belts are in black and brown, so I try to make them match up. If I'm wearing a brown belt, I'll always be wearing brown shoes to match. If I drive an open car to work and it's cold out in the morning, I have to have a coat on.

What and when is your first drink in the morning?

When I walk in the door at work, I grab a cup of coffee. I love coffee. I can't think of anything I like more than coffee. So I'll come into the plant, go down to the company lunchroom, and I'll get a cup of coffee and sit down at the piano in anticipation of Nancy (my assistant) getting here. And I'll play the piano. We have two pianos, side by side, so when Nancy gets in and hears the piano play when she comes through the door, she'll come on down, sit at the second piano beside me, and she and I will play for about twenty minutes. We play Dixieland-type jazz, that kind of thing.

What happens if you fail?

It doesn't influence me. I can handle it. When you get to be close to ninety years old, you better be able to be flexible. I have so many interests, I can sit and read a book, I can play the piano, I have tons of wonderful people that I've been working with for thirty or forty years now who have my interests at heart. I have a good thing. I don't really have a problem.

OVER TO YOU

"The kitchen is always cleaned and the house tidied before we go to bed. It's hard to fit it in, but gratifying to wake up to a peaceful environment."

—JAMES FREEMAN, FOUNDER OF BLUE BOTTLE COFFEE

Not only does your evening routine trickle down naturally into your morning, Dutch project manager Marjolein Verbeek goes as far as to say that her evening and morning routines seem inseparable: "It almost feels like my sleep is part of a daily, twelve-hour-long routine," she told us.

We know that not everyone can afford to bask in candlelight and head to bed early. Some of us work later than others, and some work night shifts that equate the beginning of our evening with the beginning of our workday. That said, if you are home by a reasonable hour, you might find that you can use your evening not only to get a head start on your morning routine, but also to enjoy an evening routine in and of itself.

Here are some activities to consider bringing into your evening:

LAY OUT YOUR CLOTHES FOR THE NEXT DAY

Reducing decision fatigue (see page 79 for more on this) in the morning has a huge payoff for your emotional health. When you lay out your clothes for the next day the night before, that's one less choice you have to make upon waking.

"Every Sunday night, I look at my calendar and the weather for the week and pick out my outfits for each day. This gives me one less thing to think about in the mornings."

—TERRA CARMICHAEL, VICE PRESIDENT OF GLOBAL COMMUNICATIONS AT EVENTBRITE

If you work out first thing in the morning, laying out your workout clothes reduces the chance of you flaking on your exercise. When you wake up, you don't have to decide whether to put them on or not; the past version of yourself has already made the decision for you. Similarly, consider showering or taking a bath in the evening. Not only will this relax you before bed, doing so in the evening will save you time in the morning.

MAKE A TO-DO LIST FOR THE NEXT DAY, AND CHECK YOUR CALENDAR

This tip should be heeded at the end of your workday rather than just before going to bed, so as not to ruin your wind-down ritual. When you make a to-do list for the next day and check your calendar, you know that when you start work in the morning you can get right down to business.

This is similar in part to the shutdown ritual, as proposed by Cal Newport in *Deep Work*. The shutdown ritual, in Newport's own words, works as follows:

"Ensure that every incomplete task, goal, or project has been reviewed and that for each you have confirmed that either (1) you have a plan you trust for its completion, or (2) it's captured in a place where it will be revisited when the time is right. The process should be an algorithm: a series of steps you always conduct, one after another. When you're done, have a set phrase you say that indicates completion (to end my own ritual, I say, "Shutdown complete"). This final step sounds cheesy, but it provides a simple cue to your mind that it's safe to release work-related thoughts for the rest of the day."

Newport notes further that: "Trying to squeeze a little more work out of your evenings might reduce your effectiveness the next day enough that you end up getting less done than if you had instead respected a shutdown."

Author and nutritionist Isabel De Los Rios adds that: "Before I end my workday, I put a sticky note on my computer that tells me exactly what I'm supposed to be writing the next morning, so that when I wake up I'm not as tempted to go right to my emails or waste time on the internet. This simple strategy really helps me focus early in the morning."

Your mind is continuously whirring with thoughts and ideas, some of which you can safely ignore, but some you need to remember. Don't let these thoughts live (and die) in your mind. Write them down.

MEDITATE, PRAY, AND JOURNAL

You don't have to do any of these things, but if any one of them speaks to you, then don't let the thought get away; they can be excellent ways to wind down, reflect on your day, and practice gratitude.

If you read our chapter on morning meditation you'll know that when we speak of meditation we mean it in both the traditional sense and in the sense of gaining more mindful moments throughout your day. For this reason, having a strict rule to remove all electronic devices from the bedroom in the evening, as we'll talk about in the Sleep chapter, will help you find these meditative moments more often.

CLEAN UP AROUND YOUR HOME

Waking up to a clean home is one of life's joys. Gracy Obuchowicz told us: "My mother taught me never to go to bed with dirty dishes in the sink, and I uphold her wisdom." We couldn't agree more.

There's something jarring about waking up to a sink full of dirty dishes, especially if you live in a small space and you spot your only pan at the bottom of the pile—the same pan you need to make breakfast.

Cleaning up your home, particularly your kitchen, before going to bed not only makes waking up the next day more pleasant, it can almost become a routine itself. While you're in the kitchen, why not set up your coffee machine so it's ready to go in the morning right before you wake up, or put out any bowls or plates you may need the next morning?

LET TECHNOLOGY LEND A HELPING HAND

Not all uses of technology in your evening routine are bad. As you just read, Nir Eyal configured his wireless router to shut off his internet connection at 10:00 P.M. to encourage him to hit the hay.

Similarly, some of the people we spoke to said they set an alarm to go off in the evening instructing them to start their evening routine.

REVERSAL

There is no reversal to creating a calm, relaxed environment to be in before going to bed, but the time in which this takes place can be fluid.

If you work a night shift, or choose to get your best work done late into the night, then just as your morning routine may begin at 3:00 or 4:00 P.M. every day, your evening routine will also take place much later in the night, or early in the morning just before you go to sleep.

CHAPTER 6

SLEEP

The Quality of Your Sleep Has a Dramatic Impact on Your Morning Routine

IT'S THE EARLY BIRD WHO SLEPT
7-9 HOURS THAT GETS THE WORM

When we were kids, bedtime was a major talking point. It was command from on high, and we waited for whatever mystical logic determined how late we could stay up to parcel out another one-hour increment.

If you're anything like us, your bedtime as an adult is rarely consistent. In this chapter, we will be looking at the morning and nighttime routines of people who, though they may not have it all figured out, have gone some way to improve the quality of their sleep and to wake up with more energy to take on their mornings. Whether or not you have a good night's sleep directly impacts your ability to perform (and enjoy) your morning routine to the best of your abilities. Don't skimp on sleep.

In this chapter we'll speak with (among others) Arianna Huffington about her habit of "gently escorting" her electronic devices out of her bedroom before going to sleep; Japanese organizing consultant Marie Kondo about the one thing she always does before going to bed; and venture capitalist Brad Feld on why he obsessively tracks his sleep every night.

ARIANNA HUFFINGTON

Founder of the *Huffington Post* and Thrive Global

When a painful wake-up call prompts you
to start taking sleep seriously.

What is your morning routine?

Ninety-five percent of the time I get eight hours of sleep a night, and as a result, 95 percent of the time I don't need an alarm to wake up. And waking up naturally is, for me, a great way to start the day.

A big part of my morning routine is about what I don't do: when I wake up, I don't start the day by looking at my phone. Instead, once I'm awake, I take a minute to breathe deeply, be grateful, and set my intention for the day.

How long have you stuck with this routine? What has changed?

I really began to take my morning routine seriously after my painful wake-up call in 2007, when I fainted from sleep deprivation and exhaustion, hit my head on my desk, and broke my cheekbone.

I've made small changes over time; for example, when I lived in Los Angeles I was fond of morning walks and hikes. I'm very open to experimenting—I'm sure before long I'll learn about something new I'll want to add to my routine.

What time do you go to sleep?

Most nights I'm in bed by 11:00 P.M., and my goal, as we joke in my family, is to always be in bed to catch the "midnight train."

Do you do anything before bed to make your morning easier?

I treat my transition to sleep as a sacrosanct ritual. First, I turn off all my electronic devices and gently escort them out of my bedroom. Then, I take a hot bath with Epsom salts and a candle flickering nearby—a bath that I prolong if I'm feeling anxious or worried about something. I don't sleep in my workout clothes as I used to (think of the mixed message that sends to our brains), but have pajamas, nightdresses, and even T-shirts dedicated to sleep. Sometimes I have a cup of chamomile or lavender tea if I want something warm and comforting before going to bed. I love reading real, physical books, especially poetry, novels, and books that have nothing to do with work.

Can you tell us more about why you don't use an alarm?

I love waking up without an alarm. Just think about the definition of the word "alarm": "a sudden fear or distressing suspense caused by an awareness of danger; apprehension; fright," or "any sound, outcry, or information intended to warn of approaching danger." So an alarm, in most situations, is a signal that something is not right. Yet most of us rely on some kind of alarm clock, a knee-jerk call to arms, to start the day, ensuring that we emerge from sleep in full fight-or-flight mode, flooded with stress hormones and adrenaline as our body readies itself for danger.

I also don't believe in the snooze button. On days when I do have to use an alarm, I always set it for the last possible moment I have to get up.

Do you have a morning workout routine?

Thirty minutes on my stationary bike on days when I'm home; and five to ten minutes of yoga stretches. I do twenty to thirty minutes of meditation before my workout routine.

Do you answer email first thing in the morning?

I make a point not to answer email right when I wake up, and I avoid the temptation by not keeping my electronic devices charging in my room. But since I'm running a news organization, and the morning is an incredibly important time for conversations with our editors, it's important for me to be reachable. I'm on email as soon as I hit my bike.

Do you use any apps or products to enhance your morning routine?

I don't use anything to enhance my sleep that requires having my phone by my bed. I love listening to soothing guided meditations before bed, but I have them on an iPod. I have my favorites in an appendix to *The Sleep Revolution*. My best endorsement for them is that I have no idea how they end, because I always fall asleep before they finish!

Do you also follow this routine on weekends?

I follow it on weekends, too! But my exercise time and meditation are longer.

What happens if you fail?

Being committed to a routine is, of course, what makes it a routine. That said, on some days life intervenes or we get off track. And when this happens, I try not to judge myself or let it negatively influence the rest of my day.

I'm a big proponent of silencing the voice of self-judgment and self-doubt in our heads, which I call the obnoxious roommate. It's the voice that feeds on putting us down and strengthening our insecurities and doubts. I have spent many years trying to evict my obnoxious roommate and have now managed to relegate her to only occasional guest appearances in my head!

MARIE KONDO
Author of *The Life-Changing Magic of Tidying Up*

When your morning is thrown off if you
leave the house without tidying perfectly.

What is your morning routine?

I wake up around 6:30 in the morning. I open the windows to let in some fresh air, and I purify the house by burning incense.

I like to have warm drinks like hot water or herbal tea before I eat breakfast. My husband often makes breakfast about an hour after I wake up; it's usually something simple like toast and eggs, or rice and miso soup. We'll then pray before our home shrine together to give thanks and imagine our days to be good ones. Sometimes, I practice yoga.

How long have you stuck with this routine? What has changed?

I've been opening the windows in my house to let in fresh air since I was a child. I began burning incense about two years ago. Previously, wiping the tataki, a place for removing shoes in a Japanese entranceway, was part of my daily morning routine, but ever since I had my first daughter, I've become busier and have had less of a chance to regularly clean that area.

What time do you go to sleep?

Around 11:30 P.M. Before going to bed I'll often rub aromatic essential oils on the back of my neck, which helps me have a good sleep. I also tidy the house by putting everything back in their designated places.

Do you use an alarm to wake up?

I rarely use an alarm. I only use it when I'm especially tired and have something that I need to do the next morning.

What happens if you fail?

It usually doesn't influence the rest of my day, unless I have to leave the house before I have finished tidying perfectly. When this happens, it's on my mind the whole day.

JON GOLD

Interdisciplinary designer and engineer

When it's hard to reform after you spent
your twenties as a night owl.

What is your morning routine?

The short version is I wake up at 6:30 A.M., try to stay away from anything with an LCD screen, meditate, exercise, and set myself up to live my best life.

What time do you go to sleep?

I'm in bed by 10:00 P.M. most days. I read a book for a while and go to sleep around 11:00.

Backstory: I was a night owl for the longest time. Once I tried tracking "go to bed by midnight" on a habit-tracking app and gave up because I never, ever managed to do it. I went to bed sometime between midnight and 4:00 A.M. for most of my twenties.

Lots of factors contributed to this: living in Europe (the American internet was on fire when I was trying to get to bed); freelancing from home or coffee shops; and, honestly, having limited self-control. That said, I've observed the benefits of being a morning person for years, and I think I'm finally making it happen.

It's easy to make bad decisions when we have low energy and rapidly decreasing willpower. Prior to becoming a morning person I noticed that I tended to stay up all night doing nothing at all productive on the internet—if I was on my laptop at 11:30 P.M., I'd probably be on it until 2:30 A.M. I fixed this by using pretty aggressive content blocks* on my laptop to block anything vaguely related to social media, entertainment, or news from 10:00 P.M. until 11:00 A.M. (and again at regular intervals during the day). I keep blocking distractions until 11:00 in the morning because that's another low-willpower time of day for me; if I groggily start checking the internet in the morning, I set myself up to have a bad day. Similarly, I charge anything with an LCD screen in my living

---

* For a frequently updated list of the latest content blockers available, head on over to mymorningroutine.com/products.

room overnight. The only device I allow in my bedroom is my Kindle. Even with content blockers on my computer and phone, those devices are too distracting to let me get a good night's sleep—I don't want to be tempted to wake up in the middle of the night to see my notifications.

Do you do anything before bed to make your morning easier?

I wear the exact same outfit every day; my closet has a few sets of identical clothes so that mornings are super quick. If I'm working out in the morning, I set out my clothes by my bed so I don't have to think about them.

When I'm winding down in the evening I write the next day's schedule in my notebook. I got this technique from *Deep Work* by Cal Newport, one of the best books I've read this year. I've always had a problem with focus, so I like to help myself out as much as possible. It's empowering to wake up and not have to use my morning brain to think about the order in which I'm supposed to do things.

Do you have a morning meditation routine?

Yes! I find that meditation is the main, key habit for my having a good life. That sounds dramatic, but I absolutely mean it.

I primarily practice Vipassanā meditation; occasionally I'll practice Mettā meditation in the evening to change things up. I've had a variety of guided and unguided stints; currently I'm using Dan Harris's wonderful 10% Happier app, which has excellent guided meditations from some of the best teachers around.

Two of the most influential meditation books for me were Harris's *10% Happier* (surprise!) and Bhante Gunaratana's

Mindfulness in Plain English. I'd also recommend going on a retreat if you want to take your practice further—ten-day silent retreats are daunting, but weekend retreats are convenient and super refreshing.

BRAD FELD
Venture capitalist at Foundry Group

When you divide your day into
"introverted" and "extroverted" parts.

What is your morning routine?

Five years ago, I woke up at 5:00 every morning during the week, regardless of what time zone I was in. On the weekends, I'd sleep until I woke up, often logging over twelve hours of sleep on Saturday and Sunday nights. Then I had a major depressive episode and decided to stop waking up with an alarm clock. I now get up whenever I wake up, which is anywhere between 5:30 and 9:00 A.M.

My morning routine is simple. I go to the bathroom, weigh myself, brush my teeth, and make a cup of coffee. I sit with my wife, Amy, wherever in the house she and the dogs are (they usually wake up before me). We like to do a ritual we call "four minutes in the morning," where we just sit with our coffee, talk a little, and watch the day open up and the birds sing.

Next, I open my laptop, still sitting wherever Amy and the dogs are, write a blog post, and do some email. I run four to five times a week, so if it's a running day, that's next. I take a shower after my run, eat something light (a smoothie or a piece of toast and peanut butter), and then start the extroverted part of my day, where I interact with other human beings.

What time do you go to sleep?

I go to sleep between 9:30 and 10:30 P.M. every night, even on the weekends. I'm rarely up later than 10:30.

Do you have a morning meditation routine?

I go through phases where I'll do twenty minutes of silent meditation in the morning. I view meditation as "practice," so I don't try to either get good at it or do it every day. Rather than "inconsistent," I'd describe my practice as "streaky."

Do you use any apps or products to enhance your morning routine?

Several years ago I started using a CPAP (Continuous Positive Airway Pressure) machine. I have a minor sleep apnea, and the CPAP machine has been life changing for me.

What are your most important tasks in the morning?

Spending time with Amy and the dogs.

What and when is your first drink in the morning?

Coffee, which I usually have within fifteen minutes of waking up. I limit myself to one a day.

Do you also follow this routine on weekends?

I do a digital Sabbath on most Saturdays, when I don't look at email, my phone, or the web all day. On Sundays, I sit with Amy after I get up and read the *New York Times*. I usually run on Saturdays and Sundays (and do long runs on those days), so my morning is quiet, mellow, and devoid of stimuli from external data.

SCOTT ADAMS
Creator of the *Dilbert* comic strip

When you're happiest, smartest, most creative,
and most optimistic between 4:00 and 8:00 A.M.

What is your morning routine?

My routine changes over time. If you threw a dart at my time-
line it would always be a little different, but there are some
things that don't change.

One is that I get up as early as I can, assuming I've had
enough sleep. Recently I've been getting up between 4:00 and
6:00 A.M. I'm experimenting with my energy by not using an
alarm clock and just making sure I get up between those times.
I'm trading the loss of a little time in the morning with that of
getting a little extra sleep on the days when my body demands
it, then seeing if my higher energy during the day pays for the
extra hour I lost due to sleep. I've been doing this for a few
months and I don't know the outcome of the experiment just
yet. You have to live with it for a while before you know.

Some people are just morning people, myself included, so
for me not only is it easy to get up in the morning, that's the
best part of my day. Typically speaking I'm happiest, smartest, most creative, and most optimistic between the hours of
4:00 and 8:00 A.M.

How long have you stuck with this routine? What has changed?

The bare bones of it is that I always go to work as soon as I get
up; I tend to do all my creative work before 10:00 because my

energy changes then, I need to get out of the house after that much work, so I'll get in my car and head to the gym. Of course, life gets in the way a lot; there are some things you just can't schedule, but in general I stick to that about 80 percent of the time.

When I was working at Pacific Bell and working on *Dilbert* on the side, I would try to be in bed by 10:00 P.M. and I found I could go pretty long periods with five or six hours of sleep a night without feeling it, as I would frequently wake up at 4:00 to draw before my commute to work.

During this time I was lucky in that my daily activities were compatible. It used to be that I'd go to work and I'd become frustrated if something went wrong, or somebody acted how I didn't want them to act. But once I became a cartoonist I had this strange situation in which everything bad that happened to me during my day made it easier to draw my cartoon. That became the topic for the next day. So my attitude shifted to "This is good; please do some more of this stupid stuff" so I could have more material for my cartoons. In this same vein, I once read some advice from Stephen King in his book *On Writing*, in which he mentioned that if you want to be a writer it's good to get a job like working as a security guard, for example night security, where you're just sitting there mindlessly staring into space for eight hours a day.

What time do you go to sleep?

I'm trying to get to bed at 11:00 P.M. During those years while I was working two jobs, getting up at 4:00 A.M. and getting done at 10:00 P.M., the moment my head hit the pillow I would be sound asleep, which is a clear sign of sleep deprivation. Being tired can be dangerous; it takes a pretty predictable chunk off your IQ. As an example, if you have a nice lofty IQ of 120, you're going to operate at 110 if you're sleepy.

Do you do anything before bed to make your morning easier?

Everything is done before I go to bed. I'm a world-class compartmentalizer. People always ask me, "Do you think about your comic all day long, what you're going to draw, looking for ideas?" and the answer is, "No, I don't think of it once," I think of it when I'm sitting down to do it, and that's it.

The worst thing you can do if you're trying to get to sleep is to make a list of what you have to do tomorrow in your head. I have a seven-second rule in my house, which is that I have to be within seven seconds of a pen and piece of paper, because that's how long I can hold a thought before I'm interrupted.

How soon after waking up do you have breakfast?

I used to eat a banana in the morning, but I stopped because I didn't like the glycemic index, so now I usually have a protein bar and a coffee. I don't do anything else until I have the coffee and protein bar in my hand. I'll then last on the protein bar for several hours. If I'm hungry by midmorning I'll have some fruit or nuts, or an avocado or something to snack on.

Do you have a morning meditation routine?

I don't. I'm a trained hypnotist, and when I learned hypnosis I learned that self-hypnosis, if you're trained to do it, is more effective and faster than meditation.

Do you answer email first thing in the morning?

It turns out that the worst thing you can do with an email is answer it, because you get more back.

I actually took a tip from my old philosophy teacher, who said that when somebody puts something in his inbox, the first thing he does is leave it there for two weeks. When he does this, one of two things happens. After two weeks somebody says, "Well it wasn't that important, we took care of it some other way," or they say, "It's still important," in which case he knows it really was important and he does something about it.

Do you use any apps or products to enhance your morning routine?

I don't, but I have a theory that there's only one thing you need to track, and if you tracked it, it would tell you how effective somebody is, and how healthy (physically and mentally) they are. And that's their sleep.

I'll bet that if we had trackers of these sorts, and we came into a meeting and yours was showing that you had underslept, you know what I would do? I would cancel the meeting. Because it's going to be a waste of time. If somebody has anxiety, high stress levels, or even a medical problem, you're going to see it in their sleep. Some people are either going to sleep too much or at the wrong times, or they're going to sleep too little, but I'll bet that if you could measure that one thing, sleep, you would get every other variable you needed.

When do you check your phone?

The phone is always in my hand, but I don't get phone calls because I've trained people not to call me by ten years of dedicated not answering the phone.

Do you also follow this routine on weekends?

I wake up at the same time and work in the mornings every weekend, and part of the reason I do this is because my body doesn't know anything about getting up and working, so as soon as you say to yourself, "Is this a day I work, or is this a day I can relax?" you end up in a battle with yourself. So my weekend routine is pretty much identical, with a little less communication involved. I'll be in front of my computer working on either my book or comics. I'm always working on one of those two things.

What happens if you're traveling?

When I travel, even for vacation, I'm usually up three to four hours before the people I'm with. I don't enjoy sleeping in, so I don't. I used to stack up my daily cartoons in advance when I went on vacation, but now I have a portable drawing tablet, so I can do at least the sketching and writing for my cartoons while I'm away.

And if you fail?

It ruins my entire day, which is why it almost never happens. I'm pretty adamant about that.

Every once in a while, I think it has happened no more than twice in the last year, I'll oversleep. I'll wake up at my usual time and I'll be too tired, and I'll fall back asleep, and it'll be 9:00 or something when I wake up again. When this happens, my whole day is just screwed. I may be okay by the evening, but nothing is right after that.

OVER TO YOU

"Mornings are such an amazing reward for
going to sleep at a reasonable hour."

—GARRICK VAN BUREN, PRODUCT STRATEGIST

There are many reasons why we don't get enough sleep at night, ranging from the obvious to the esoteric.

Going to bed too late is a clear culprit. Don't become complacent about how much sleep you need; keeping a consistent bedtime will help you keep a consistent wake-up time. Drinking caffeine and alcohol close to your bedtime is just as bad for you as you've heard. Eating a heavy meal before bed is also not ideal, as it may result in heartburn and discomfort. If there's a lot of outside noise or light coming into your bedroom, you'll need to fix this. You'll also need to allow yourself to wind down properly before bed—a busy mind makes it harder to fall asleep and negatively influences your sleep quality.

Finally, if you're still struggling to get enough sleep after addressing everything you'll read in this chapter, you may be suffering from a sleep disorder, medical condition, or the side effects of prescription medication. If you expect any of these to be true, consult your doctor.

As Jon Gold touched on in his routine: "It's easy to make bad decisions when we have low energy and rapidly decreasing willpower." You deserve to give yourself the best shot at your morning routine, and the best way to do that is by making sure you're well rested.

There are many ways to achieve this, and we suggest you partner this chapter with the Evening Routines chapter to get the full picture of our recommendations for getting the most out of your mornings by making the most of your evenings and having the best night's sleep you can. Here are our tips:

WAKE UP EASIER BY GOING TO BED EARLIER

If you have trouble getting up on time in the morning, going to bed earlier is the simplest solution. Don't cheat yourself of the full benefits of your morning routine the next day.

If you tend to work late into the evening it's a good idea to experiment with this for a few weeks to see if going to bed earlier and waking up earlier works better for you. In the words of British software developer Dan Counsell: "While I get a lot done late at night, I always pay for it the next day as I often feel tired and grouchy. As I've gotten older I've realized how important sleep is. I now know how closely it's linked to my health, mood, and general focus. Getting enough sleep is the best productivity hack I know."

You should also experiment with keeping a consistent sleep schedule, getting up at the same time every day, even on weekends. Soon your body will fall into sync with this natural rhythm, and waking up at the same time every day will be a cinch.

CREATE THE PERFECT SLEEP ENVIRONMENT

One way to make it easier for you to fall asleep at night (and thus allow you to sleep longer) is by optimizing your bedroom for sleep, not wakefulness. There are many things you can do here, including:

1. Keeping your bedroom dark. Very dark. Despite all the good that electric lighting has brought us, artificial lights are the enemy of a good night's sleep. Our bodies haven't had enough time to adapt to and evolve with the number of artificial lights littering our homes and outside environments. Block out outside light with heavy curtains, or wear a sleep mask.

2. Keeping the noise down. Loud noises throughout the night (which are especially prevalent if you live in a big city) can disturb your sleep even if they don't wake you up. Consider using earplugs or blocking out noise with a fan or white-noise machine.

3. Making sure your room temperature is conducive to a good night's sleep. Sleeping in a cool environment is so beneficial to a good night's sleep that there's a popular treatment for insomnia known as "passive body heating," in which you take a hot bath an hour or two before your bedtime to raise your core body temperature. The change in your body temperature (as you cool down after your hot bath) makes you sleepy as you expend excess energy to make such a temperature drop possible—making this a popular nighttime wind-down ritual. The same sleepiness occurs if you take an ice-cold bath, as it's the energy needed to bring your body back to its core body temperature that causes your sleepiness, rather than the temperature of the bath itself.

4. Having a comfortable mattress. We cannot stress this enough. While you don't have to spend a fortune on the latest and greatest available, considering how much of your life you spend laid across this thing, and the fact that you only get one back, it's worth splurging.

HOW TO (TEMPORARILY) COPE WITH LESS SLEEP

We're purposely not using the word "thrive" or "be more pro-ductive" here because when you're getting less sleep than you need, all you can hope to do is cope. In truth, though many of us want to believe we can get by on six, or even just five hours of sleep a night, for most of us this simply isn't the case. We can all get by on less sleep, for sure (new parents do this all the time), but we cannot train our bodies to need less sleep while still functioning at our full capacity.

> "To be honest, I'm usually pretty worn out by the end of the day. Reading helps bring me to the brink of sleep very quickly."
>
> —JEFF RAIDER, COFOUNDER OF HARRY'S

Most of us require between seven and nine hours of sleep a night. Of the several hundred people we have interviewed about their morning routines, their sleep times have averaged out at seven hours and twenty-nine minutes per night, as of this book going to print. If you're consistently trying to get by on less than seven hours of sleep it *will* catch up with you, likely sooner rather than later.

With that said, people who can function perfectly well on five or six hours of sleep *do* exist (they're appropriately re-ferred to as "short sleepers"), but they are so uncommon that we can say with confidence that if you think you fall into this category, you almost certainly do not.

Of course, the truth is that from time to time we won't hit our sweet spot in the seven-to-nine-hour range (remember, that's the average; you may be on the higher end). In these cases, we recommend taking short daytime naps to help catch you up on your sleep. There are two types of naps we suggest:

1. **Power naps (10–20 minutes):** Power naps of between ten and twenty minutes are a form of napping deliberately designed to get the maximum possible efficiency from your nap, or more "bang for your buck," as Dr. Leon Lack, professor of psychology at Flinders University, Australia, describes it. During a power nap you'll remain in stage-two light sleep (stage one is falling asleep), which may include a small amount of non-rapid eye movement (NREM). Waking from a power nap should leave you feeling alert and energized, while often unsure whether you fell asleep or not.

2. **Full sleep-cycle naps (90 minutes):** A nap of ninety minutes, or one full sleep cycle, can help to reduce your sleep deficit if you're feeling sleep deprived, especially when it's taken in the 1:00 to 3:00 P.M. window. During a full-cycle nap you'll experience every sleep stage, starting in stage two (light sleep, NREM), moving to stages three and four (deep, slow-wave sleep), before reaching rapid eye movement (REM) sleep, the dream phase. The sleep stages will then reverse until you're back in stage two, at which point your 90-minute alarm should be due to go off, allowing you to avoid sleep inertia—that feeling of grogginess (and a desperate desire to go back to sleep) experienced after being woken up.

AVOID DRINKING CAFFEINE BEFORE BED

Far too many of us, ourselves included, drink caffeinated drinks such as coffee, tea, or energy drinks late into the afternoon and, as a result, find it hard to fall asleep at night. We'll then wake up the next morning, still tired from our lack of sleep, and immediately brew ourselves a new drink and start the cycle all over again. In the words of coach Melody Wilding: "[I was] Band-Aiding my exhaustion with caffeine."

We enjoy our coffee and tea as much as the next person, but we've personally discovered the benefits of not drinking them past a certain point in the afternoon. If you want to have a hot drink in the evening or right before going to bed, there are many caffeine-free herbal teas that not only won't keep you awake, they may provide just what you need to help you fall asleep.

REMOVE ELECTRONIC DEVICES FROM THE BEDROOM

Blue light (the color that comes off our phones, tablets, and computer screens) shifts the rhythm of our circadian clock, blocking melatonin production and helping us to stay awake and alert via an increase in reaction times and continued activation in areas of our brain that would otherwise be slowing down and preparing for a less active role during sleep.

Blue light is so harmful to sleep that "blue-light therapy" is a treatment for people suffering from seasonal affective disorder (also known as winter depression), helping to pep them up by having them sit in front of a light box for several sessions each day. While blue light filters are now widely available for most of our devices, these features merely "filter," that is, reduce, the amount of blue light getting through; they don't eliminate it.

Instead of sitting in bed checking email and social media on your phone right before going to sleep, only to repeat this same cycle as soon as you wake up, consider spending this time reading a book (fiction, or anything that is not work related) instead. And if you're wondering how you're going to wake up if your phone, which very likely also functions as your alarm, has been moved to another room, embrace this fact and the wakeful benefits it brings,* or consider purchasing an analog alarm clock. Benjamin's wife bought him one for his birthday last year and both of their phones have spent the night outside of their bedroom ever since.

USE WEEKENDS TO CATCH UP ON SLEEP

While we advocate trying your best to get the sleep you need every night in order to set your body on a proper sleep schedule, this isn't always possible. Technology writer Ben Brooks notes: "On the weekend I don't work, so I spend all morning with the kids. I will still get up before them if we have plans for the day, but if there are no plans I'll tend to sleep in an extra hour."

Decide whether the trade-off of getting up early on weekends to complete your morning routine is worth not getting as much sleep as a result. Take these words by author Jon Acuff to heart: "I'd say I feel less motivated and more stressed out on the days I don't exercise or get good sleep. Sleep is

---

* More on this on page 181.

critical. There are so many silly entrepreneurs who say 'Sleep when you're dead! Hustle 24/7' but that's not the recipe for success, that's the recipe for burnout and divorce. Rest is a critical part of hustle. I like to say that in a world that praises busyness, rest is an act of bravery."

REVERSAL

There is no reversal to getting enough sleep.

CHAPTER 7

PARENTS

How to Keep Up a Semblance of a Morning Routine with an Army of Kids in Tow

MORNING ROUTINE PRE-KIDS

MORNING ROUTINE AFTER KIDS

If you're a parent, you deserve to have a positive, productive morning routine just as much as the rest of us. If you don't have kids, this section is still a fun read, as many of the points mentioned can be translated to your own routine.

We'll preface this chapter by saying that neither of us are parents yet. But all the following morning routines come from parents just like you who are trying to figure things out as they go along, and who are trying to alter their morning routines to fit in with the changing needs of their kids and their family.

In this chapter we'll speak with (among others) the co-founder of Twitter, Biz Stone, on why playing with his son is his most important morning task; the founder of Cupcakes and Cashmere, Emily Schuman, on how having a baby helped her to become more routine-oriented and focused in the morning; and author and journalist Nick Bilton on how chasing his toddler around the house has become his post-kids workout routine . . .

BIZ STONE

Cofounder of Twitter and Medium

When playing with your son first thing in the morning
is the only meditation you need.

What is your morning routine?

My five-year-old son, Jake, wakes me up at 6:30 or 7:00 A.M.
The first thing I do is play with him. Our go-to for a couple of
years has been Legos. However, he recently discovered Mine-
craft for iPad. We can play that together over our local area
network (LAN), so it's just me and him in the game. We often like to play in creative mode, which means nothing bad
can happen to us and we have everything we want to build
amazing things.

After playing with my son for about an hour or so, I get
dressed. This takes very little time because I have a uniform
of a sort. I wear jeans, a black T-shirt, and blue Converse
every day so there's no need to spend time selecting an outfit. I help Jake get dressed as well. Once I'm dressed, my wife
often makes us a simple, light breakfast (sometimes oatmeal,
fruit, or toast with avocado), and then I head to work in the
city, dropping Jake off at school on the way.

How long have you stuck with this routine? What has changed?

I've been playing with my son upon waking up since he was
born. My routine has changed very little since he came along.

Do you use an alarm to wake up?

I don't use an alarm because my son is my alarm and I generally wake up at the same time naturally at this point. I only use an alarm if I have to travel and I need to wake up super early to get to the airport.

Do you have a morning meditation routine?

It's wake up and straight to it for me—no meditation. Unless playing with my son can be considered a kind of meditation.

When do you check your phone?

I don't check my phone in the morning. I just unplug it and put it on the shelf near the door so I won't forget it, along with my keys and wallet. Sometimes I will try to look at my iPad after breakfast for five minutes just to make sure I haven't missed any big news items.

What and when is your first drink in the morning?

I fill up a big bottle of water and drink the whole bottle first thing. My doctor once told me that everybody is underhydrated so I started doing that years ago. After that, I drink coffee.

What happens if you're traveling?

If I wake up in a hotel because I'm on a business trip my whole routine is thrown off and I don't know what to do with myself. In those cases, I usually tell myself I have to make a plan and stick to it. Otherwise, I'm rudderless.

And if you fail?

If I don't get a chance to play with my son in the morning I feel like I missed something that I'll never get back. It's such a joy to wake up and be in the mind-set of a five-year-old before transitioning into the role of "executive."

EMILY SCHUMAN
Founder of Cupcakes and Cashmere

When you spend your morning giving your child all the love, time, and attention she deserves.

What is your morning routine?

I wake up at around 6:00 every morning. I never use an alarm (unless I have a crazy early flight to catch). Though I find the idea of blackout shades very appealing, my husband and I keep our shades open so the sun filters in through the windows.

I say hi to my husband, then check my email. I used to go on my social media channels, but I find that I get sucked into a half-hour cycle instead of simply focusing on the present. I get up, splash water on my face, and put on a serum, lotion, and sunscreen before brushing my teeth. I get dressed in yoga pants and a sweatshirt and go into Sloan's (my two-year-old daughter) room. She wakes up anywhere from 6:00 to 7:00 A.M., so she certainly dictates my schedule a bit. I hang out in her room with her for a bit, since she likes to take her time before getting out of bed, and oftentimes I'll read her a couple of books while she just kind of lies in her crib. I then get her dressed and make her breakfast. I used to feed her similar to how I like to eat, but I've since come to realize that kids like variety. So I'll prepare her a waffle with yogurt, cut up some fruit, and add some Cheerios on the side.

After Sloan finishes up her breakfast, we'll put on some music (lately it's the *Moana* soundtrack) and play in her pretend kitchen. We make "cookies," "pasta," and "soup" most mornings and occasionally will draw or bring out the Play-Doh. Our nanny arrives at 8:30, at which point I duck back into my room to put on my makeup, brush my teeth, and get dressed. I'll then give Sloan a kiss and head out the door.

How long have you stuck with this routine? What has changed?

About a year and a half. I've always been an early riser, but the focus has certainly shifted since having a kid. I used to be a lot more spontaneous with my mornings and less routine oriented. But kids really thrive on routine (as do I, in fact), so it's been a nice change. Once she starts preschool, we'll have a little less time for reading and playing in the morning, but I still intend on creating a tranquil, happy environment before leaving the house.

Do you do anything before bed to make your morning easier?

If I'm going to a workout class (which I aim to do twice a week), I'll lay out my gym clothes ahead of time, just so I don't have to make any decisions before 7:00 A.M. On days I'm not working out, I'll occasionally make a big batch of oatmeal or granola so breakfast is already done.

Can you tell us more about why you don't use an alarm?

I've been a morning person for my entire life. Back when people had landlines when I was younger, my friends' parents used to give me times for when I was allowed to call, because otherwise I was ringing them at 5:30 A.M. On the rare occasion that I need to get up with an alarm, I never hit the snooze button. I don't think I ever have! It's not even that I don't want to keep sleeping, but more so that I'm terrified I'll fall back asleep and miss whatever it is that I'm getting up early for in the first place.

What are your most important tasks in the morning?

Making sure Sloan is well fed and feels like I've devoted my love, time, and attention to her. And that I've had my coffee.

How does your partner fit into your morning?

My husband and I alternate days when we each take care of Sloan in the morning. So on my days, he can do what he wants. Sometimes that means he's hanging out with us, occasionally he'll stay in bed, but most often he gets to the gym in time for an early class.

Do you also follow this routine on weekends?

Having a toddler means we never really sleep in, but because it's never been something my husband and I were good at, it hasn't been that rough a transition. I don't end up putting on makeup and getting dressed, instead opting for loungewear for most of the day. And since our nanny doesn't come on the weekends, it means that we head out on adventures (our current go-to spots include the beach, a trampoline park, a farm, the zoo, the aquarium, or the carousel and ponies in Griffith Park) at the time she'd normally arrive.

What happens if you fail?

A few weeks back, on one of my husband's mornings, I woke up at 5:30 and started reading in bed. I assumed I'd simply get up with him and hang out until it was time to get ready for work. But somehow I managed to fall back asleep and slept in until 8:20—that's a big deal when you have a two-year-old. It felt so luxurious, and even though I had to speed up the rest of my morning because of it, it was a welcome surprise and a nice reminder that it's important to occasionally take time for myself.

AMANDA HESSER
CEO of Food52, cookbook author

When you employ your significant other as a human alarm clock.

What is your morning routine?

Because I sleep through any alarm, my husband, Tad, kindly wakes me up. That's usually around 6:45 A.M. I'm glacially slow to wake so I can't just hop out of bed.

After I finally open my eyes, which takes five to ten minutes (my eyelids feel so heavy!), I like to read the news on my phone to get my brain engaged. Once I manage to slide myself out of bed (which is usually when I hear Tad's footfalls coming toward our room to check on me), I drink a large glass of water. This wakes up my senses. I've also convinced myself that it washes away any impurities from sleep.

Tad makes our ten-year-old twins breakfast and reads aloud to them while they eat; I'm usually ambling into the kitchen at about this time. I make our kids' lunches and listen to whatever story is in progress; right now it's Lord of the Rings. Once their lunches are packed, I spend five or ten minutes doing yoga and then take a very hot shower. The last fifteen minutes of getting ready usually involve me running late and scrambling out the door with kids in tow and bags and sunglasses not quite on.

What time do you go to sleep?

I used to be such a night owl and wouldn't become productive until about 11:00 P.M., after which I would happily work until 2:00 A.M. That made for some very rough mornings.

About three years ago this changed suddenly and drastically. I found myself much less resilient without a good night's sleep, and I simply got tired earlier. At first I thought I was dying, of course, but over time I've come to appreciate my new internal clock. It's actually forced me into a much healthier sleep pattern. Now I'm in bed by 10:00 or 10:30 P.M. and asleep by 11:00.

Do you do anything before bed to make your morning easier?

Tad makes fun of me for this, but old habits die hard. When I was young I started picking out my outfits the night before school, and I still do this! I lay out everything from my underwear to my jewelry. I also pack my backpack and purse. This ritual gives me a sense of tranquillity before bedtime.

I also make sure the kitchen is tidy and ready for the next day. To me, nothing is more depressing than coming into a messy kitchen in the morning.

How soon after waking up do you have breakfast?

If I'm going directly to the office, I pick up a croissant and decaf coffee with soy milk. Let's not discuss the decaf or the soy milk; both depress me but are necessary.

I much prefer breakfast meetings to lunch meetings, so when I meet someone for breakfast I order two poached eggs, toast with butter, orange juice, and coffee. I like blunt, wholesome foods in the morning. Lunch and dinner are for whimsy.

BOB FERGUSON
Attorney general of Washington State

When your morning is reserved for those closest to you.

What is your morning routine?

I wake up between 5:00 and 6:30 every morning. My routine is simple. First, I have a little personal time—breakfast, coffee, the morning news (okay, maybe I'm checking the news a little earlier than I should). Then I wake up our nine-year-old twins, Jack and Katie—and my wife, Colleen—and I get them ready and out the door for school.

The twins wake up at 7:30 every day, almost like clockwork. I like to be the one to wake them in the morning. Katie gets right up with a smile on her face. Jack can be a little more of a project. We talk (or more likely, Katie, Colleen, and I talk while Jack finishes waking up) as Colleen and I get their breakfast ready. They like to read their books over breakfast. I'm a big believer that how your day starts is really important. It's easy for meetings to go late at work, or for other events to come up, and I'm not always guaranteed much time with them later in the day, so I like to lock in that morning time.

Do you do anything before bed to make your morning easier?

I try to avoid morning meetings so I can be home with the kids. If I do have an early meeting, I lay out all my clothes and essentials the night before so I can slip out without waking anyone.

Do you answer email first thing in the morning?

While I might be checking my phone for news early on, I try to hold off on answering messages until later in the day. The early mornings belong to my family and me.

Do you also follow this routine on weekends?

Jack and Colleen sometimes sleep in, but Katie is an early riser. I often get one-on-one time with Katie on weekend mornings. I'll come into her room and read to her until Jack wakes up, then I move to his room and read to him for a while before everyone starts their day.

JAMIE MOREA
Cofounder of Hyperbiotics and Valentia Skin Care

When you realize you're the parent of
an adorable miniature dictator.

What is your morning routine?

I'd like to take this opportunity to preface all of my morning routine answers with this simple fact: I am the mother of a breastfeeding, cosleeping toddler who apparently finds great pleasure in witnessing the demise of almost every routine I try to abide by. That said, on a glorious day after a successful night, I (we) wake up around 7:30 A.M. Because my son likes to start his morning off with milk and cuddles, we usually lie in bed for a while, which allows me to wake up slowly. Suddenly, my adorable miniature dictator realizes this is boring and he wants to play. He usually calls for our dog, Annie, to join us, and then he wants to go outside.

By this point, my lifesaver of a husband has already started making my Swiss-Water-process-decaf latte with homemade almond milk and MCT oil. I recently kicked my caffeine habit in pursuit of a more alkaline diet, but thanks to Pavlovian conditioning,* if it looks like coffee and tastes like coffee, it still works for me.

On a perfect day, husband and toddler willing, they will play outside and I'll sneak upstairs for a brief meditation and yoga session.

Becoming a parent has forced me to embrace flexibility and make the best of whatever card is dealt to me on any given day. I used to sleep eight to nine hours and start each day with yoga, meditation, and journaling. I'd clear my head and set my intentions, and I even had the audacity to be creative with my appearance. I would actually spend time fixing my hair and selecting my clothes. Ha! I know all babies are different, but the one that we got is far from passive and easygoing. I've adapted just about every part of my life to support

---

* Pavlovian conditioning, or the theory of classical conditioning, was discovered accidentally in the 1890s, when Russian physiologist Ivan Pavlov, while studying the role of saliva in dogs' digestive processes, noticed that the dogs in his study would begin to salivate in anticipation of being fed, even when no food was present.

and foster his strong and fiery personality. I know the day will come when he needs me less, and I'll be able to go back to my ideal, more structured ways.

In the meantime, it's a good thing beauty comes from within, because these days we play it by ear and turn a whole lot of lemons into delicious lemonade.

How soon after waking up do you have breakfast?

I became a big fan of intermittent fasting after learning about its impact on gut health, so I try to maximize the length of time between when I eat dinner at night and when I have my first bite in the morning. I usually succeed at a full twelve-hour stretch, and sometimes make it as long as fifteen hours.

Do you have a morning meditation routine?

I practice Vedic meditation. I attended a course several years ago that helped me develop a practice, and it has changed me from the inside out. Being able to enter such a complete sense of calm, stillness, and clarity is a superpower that we all have access to.

What are your most important tasks in the morning?

Plan with my husband how we are going to divide and conquer (usually based on who is feeling the most tired).

What happens if you fail?

I used to be really thrown when I wasn't able to start my day like I wanted. Now, I am doing my best to see it as a gift. Days when I feel off-kilter and still manage to find my alignment usually end up full of wonderful surprises.

So, rather than being frustrated at my little one for being

awake at 4:00 A.M., I try to focus on the beauty of mamahood and what an honor it is to have the precious little being fully dependent on me for a few years.

NICK BILTON
Special correspondent for *Vanity Fair*,
author of *American Kingpin*

When you spend your morning protecting the dog from
the toddler, the baby from the dog, and the toddler from himself.

What is your morning routine?

I have two morning routines. One was pre-kids, the other is post-kids.

Before we had children (we have two under two) my mornings were rather civilized. I'd wake up at around 6:00 A.M., feed the dog, make coffee, put on an old hoodie, and then I'd sit in my office and either read a book, write, or both. When I'm writing a book, or a big magazine feature, I tend to work with my wi-fi turned off and my phone in airplane mode so I don't see new mail fill my inbox or get jolted by an unimportant alert. The internet is a distraction, and if I need to look something up for the passage I'm writing, I can look it up later. (I usually have my second cup of coffee right about now.) I also find that in the morning, alone in my office without interruption, I can write more in the first couple of hours of the day than I can throughout the entire next twelve hours. Then, by around 8:30, my wife would wake up and I'd bring her a coffee in bed and take the dog for a walk.

That all changed when we had children. Now I have routine number two: I wake up at 5:30, usually being summoned into our two-year-old's room with shrieks of "Dada!" and "downstairs!" and "cartoons!" and "eggy!" I'm lucky that I don't need a lot of sleep—I can get by on five hours—but given that my wife and I have usually been woken up several times in the evening, I'm pretty bleary-eyed at this point. Then it's a whirlwind of protecting the dog from the toddler, the baby from the dog, the toddler from himself, making breakfast, drinking several cups of coffee, and chasing my son as he runs around the house and yard in circles screaming like he's in the ring at a WWF tournament. We interrupt this chaos by walking the dog together as a family (which is my new favorite part of the day). If I'm lucky, I start writing by around 9:30 A.M., when the nanny has arrived. But I often end up leaving the house to go work at a coffee shop because there's still so much chaos.

How long have you stuck with this routine? What has changed?

The first routine I stuck with for many years. Before I became a special correspondent for *Vanity Fair,* I was a reporter and columnist for the *New York Times,* and I simultaneously wrote books during my time there, so I'd wake up in the morning at 6:00, work on my book for the first two or three hours, then put that away and begin my *New York Times* work, coming back to the book editing in the evening before bed.

The new routine has been going on for exactly two years. I do think that eventually, as the kids get older, the two routines will start to blend together. But we've still got some time before that happens.

My pre-kids morning routine can best be described as sitting in a quaint old boat on a serene lake. It's a summer afternoon, and birds flitter by as a light breeze brushes the trees.

My post-kids routine is more akin to being in one of those giant cargo ships in the middle of the ocean as a nor'easter rages in the distance, creating waves that are so big they look like mountains in the middle of the sea. I love them both, to be honest. They are just very, very different mornings.

What time do you go to sleep?

I get into bed around 10:30 or 11:00 P.M., read for a little on my phone (I know, bad habit), then go to sleep thirty minutes later. I'm not overexaggerating when I say that when my head hits the pillow, it takes me just a few seconds to fall asleep.

Do you use an alarm to wake up?

No. I have a human alarm clock that gets up at 5:30 A.M. And if by chance the human alarm clock sleeps in (a rarity, but it happens), then my four-legged alarm clock will be sure to wake me up at 6:00 by wagging her tail and jabbing her wet nose in my face.

Do you have a morning workout routine?

Yes. Chasing a toddler around the house.

What and when is your first drink in the morning?

Coffee. Black. Mere minutes after I've woken up.

How does your partner fit into your morning?

My wife has usually been up a lot of the night with the little baby, so I try to let her get some rest. If she has managed to get some sleep (another rarity), then we all get up and spend time together as a family, making pancakes and going for a walk, which is frankly the best morning routine there is.

What happens if you're traveling?

When I'm traveling for work, staying in a hotel, I try my best to go back to my pre-children morning routine, getting up early and working for a couple of hours before the day begins.

Anything else you would like to add?

In my early twenties I used to think routines were no fun and were for people who didn't want to experience something new. I remember intentionally taking different routes to work each morning, or stopping at a different coffee shop every day. But as I got older, whether it's sitting alone in my office writing or chasing a two-year-old around the house, I grew to love a morning routine.

OVER TO YOU

"It's important to note that the morning routines
of parents are radically different than those
of people without kids."

—DAVE ASPREY, CREATOR OF BULLETPROOF COFFEE

From our research, Dave is right. If you had a morning routine before becoming a parent, you may have found that it fell by the wayside the moment you added a baby to the mix. Julie Zhuo confessed to us: "Before I had kids I wasn't quite as regimented about my mornings. With children there are a lot more steps."

Here is our collected advice on how to adapt to, and enjoy, your morning routine as a parent of young kids:

WAKE UP BEFORE YOUR KIDS

You need you time. Chances are, when your baby was born and first came home, you sacrificed any time for yourself in favor of keeping your child alive and well. This is a transition every new parent must go through. As WNYC Studios podcast host and author Manoush Zomorodi told us: "I was never an early riser before kids, and then when they were little I just tried to sleep whenever they slept. Why on earth would I set an alarm when I was so perpetually exhausted?! Now that we are on more of a schedule, I've decided I like accomplishing something before having to deal with all the hectic details of getting out the door for school."

This will not work for everyone, and it will depend on how well your kids sleep through the night. When taking care of a baby, we recommend prioritizing sleep over your morning routine as it is likely hard to get otherwise. But if you *can* wake up before your kids, do.

> "My pre-kid mornings seem so luxurious now! If I can actually get up and get myself totally ready before my son is up, I always feel better."
>
> —LAURA ROEDER, ENTREPRENEUR

Have your own uninterrupted time in the mornings by getting up before your kids. Don't let their wake-up time be your wake-up time, otherwise you'll never have any time to yourself. Allowing yourself this time makes it easier for you to give them your full attention when they are awake.

ADAPT YOUR MORNING ROUTINE TO YOUR KIDS' NEEDS

Norwegian artist Victoria Durnak notes: "Life with an infant is a constant negotiation of routine. We follow a routine, and then my son learns a new skill or his teeth are bothering him or he is unsettled by something or he acquires different needs, and the routine has to change." Similarly, Jamie Morea pointed out in her routine that: "Becoming a parent has forced me to embrace flexibility and make the best of whatever card is dealt to me on any given day."

As your kids grow older their own schedules will need to adapt. Adapt accordingly. In the timeless words of cofounder and president of Food52, Merrill Stubbs: "It's all about flexibility and unpredictability. I can't be too wedded to a specific routine or I'm bound to be disappointed when things go awry. I mean, poop happens. Literally."

KIDS THRIVE ON ROUTINE

Kids, much like adults, thrive on routine. Sticking to a morning routine with babies and young children is crucial for their development and general sense of well-being as they go through life.

When you travel with babies and young children, try to keep their travel routine as close to their at-home routine as possible. Planning and sticking to a routine is critical. You'll thank yourself when your kids start school: the routine of getting your kids ready for school in the morning will serve them well as they grow up.

Merrill Stubbs also notes that her most important task in the morning is: "getting everyone out the door in a timely fashion; I think the most apt metaphor for my mornings is that of being shot out of a cannon."

KEEP YOUR EYES OFF YOUR DEVICES IN THE MORNING

This is easier said than done, but we suggest making it a rule in your house that you cannot check your phone, or other devices, in the morning when your kids can see you (if you have to check your phone briefly, do so behind closed doors).

"I try to wait to check my phone until after the boys have left for school/work. It keeps me focused on my son, grounded in the moments I have with him."

—ROBYN DEVINE, ENTREPRENEUR

Doing this allows you to be more present around your kids, so you can enjoy making and eating breakfast with them, and as they get older, talking to them about their day and what they're most excited for. Your child will remember these moments as times when you were truly present together and they had your full attention.

SAY A PROPER GOOD-BYE EVERY MORNING

If you don't spend your days with your kids, ensure that their (and your) emotional well-being is in a good place every morning by saying a proper good-bye. Dan Counsell says that: "Making sure I properly say good-bye to my wife and kids" is his most important task in the morning. "Kisses, hugs, and I love yous all round. It might sound sickeningly sweet but when it comes down to it my family are the most important thing to me."

Embrace these moments, and always leave the house on a positive note.

REMEMBER, IT'S ONLY TEMPORARY

From both a positive and negative perspective, your time as a new parent is only temporary. Even if you have four or five kids, each of those moments of you being a new parent will go by in an instant. Make the most of them while they're there, and remember that once they're gone, you can return to a more you-focused morning routine.

Highrise CEO Nathan Kontny puts it simply: "I love that we get to eat and hang out and read together before she [Nathan's daughter] starts her day. It completely grounds me for the day ahead."

Having a great start to the day with your children is so important to your (and their) overall happiness. Embrace it; it is everything. Designer and author Manuel Lima notes: "Before Chloe was born, I always tried to work out and eat healthily, but too often I would work until late, then press the snooze button several times in the morning, only to run to work without having a proper meal. Chloe made me go to bed earlier, and in the process, start enjoying the quietness of early mornings and the pleasure of an unhurried first meal. Now, I don't think I could go back to my seemingly flexible but more unruly routine."

REVERSAL

There is no reversal to this. Just remember, it's only temporary.

CHAPTER 8

SELF-CARE

How to Start the Day with Gentleness

HE'LL BE IN THERE UNTIL 8 A.M.
IT'S HIS ME TIME.

If there's one thing the morning offers that no other time of day can, it's the ability to start again with a clean slate. But that clean slate can quickly become muddied by the responsibilities of the day, ruining our best-laid plans to keep a clear mind and a calm heart.

What if we were to tell you that this clean slate could stay clean for longer? That by slowing down your morning you could slow down your whole day? That you could give yourself the time and space you need to take care of your deepest needs, to start your day, as it were, with gentleness? Gentleness toward you, toward your spouse, and toward all those around you.

In this chapter we'll speak with (among others) award-winning Japanese illustrator Yuko Shimizu on why she chooses to take the slow train to work in the morning; fine artist and illustrator Lisa Congdon on how her morning routine grounds her and fuels her creativity; and Dr. John Berardi on why he spends time sitting on his kitchen counter every morning.

ELLE LUNA
Artist, author of *The Crossroads of Should and Must*

When you have a whole science for tricking yourself
into remembering your dreams.

What is your morning routine?

The first thing I do when I wake up is try to remember my dreams! Do you remember your dreams? I have this strange sense that remembering our dreams is really, really important. Dreams seem to hold all these clues and insights about what's really going on. And there have been all of these people throughout time who have learned from their dreams. Did you know Mary Shelley wrote *Frankenstein* because she dreamed it? And the tune for the song "Yesterday" by Paul McCartney was something he heard in a dream? The psychologist Carl Jung studied and shared his dreams with Sigmund Freud. And now you can even buy this incredible book called *The Book of Symbols,* based on the work of mythologist Joseph Campbell, which chronicles dreams and symbols.

One of the most effective ways I've found to capture my dreams is to use the voice recorder on my phone. While still somewhere between awake and asleep, I recount my dreams out loud. One of the things I try to do in addition to actually describing the dream is to give commentary on how the dream is making me feel. For example, I once had a dream in which this massive cobra snake appeared in front of me. Now, typically, I'd think that a snake might be a scary symbol to see in a dream, but as I was recounting this, I took care to note that this snake was majestic, that it was powerful and beautiful and that I was not afraid. I think it was Carl Jung who said that the most important aspect of our dreams is what the dreams mean to us, how we interpret them. It's not about what a dream dictionary says a symbol means or what a friend thinks, it's how we interpret them in that moment. I like that.

After I capture (and now paint) my dreams, Tilly, my cocker spaniel, and I go for a leisurely morning walk. We dillydally together, stopping a lot and looking at things.

Next up is coffee. I used to drink a couple of cups of coffee a day, but one day my neighbor Michael made me a cup of coffee that was so delicious, I'm talking so totally experientially awesome, that one cup was all I needed. Just like that, I went from being a multicupper to a single-cupper. I remember that morning watching Michael smell the beans in the bag with his eyes closed. He then walked over to me, held the bag up to my nose, and asked me, "What do you smell?" Cherries and roses! I had never taken the time to smell my coffee like that. He showed me how to be present to the entire experience—from boiling the water to enjoying the first sip. I learned a lot from watching him that day, and since then, making a warm cup of coffee in the morning has taken on a very special place in my day.

After coffee, I tend to the altar in my studio. This altar is the spiritual heartbeat of the space. When I tend to it, I feel like I am being reconnected to Bali, where I found the altar, and the women who create daily ceremonies around the altars. If you've ever been to Bali, you know firsthand that the country is riddled with altars. They're everywhere! And they're colorful and covered in fresh flowers and incense. The entire island smells of jasmine and sandalwood and fresh delicate flowers. What an experience!

I spend a good amount of time in Bali working with women batik artists for a textile project I run called the Bulan Project. When I'm there, mornings are a magical time of the day—you can hear the roosters singing and the ducks searching for breakfast in the rice paddies. Wearing their ceremonial sarongs, the women are these gorgeous slices of color moving amidst palm trees and rice paddies. They carry towering trays of handmade offerings made from meticulously braided palm leaves, fresh flowers, and packages of fresh mints and cookies. They must spend hours making these offerings daily—they're incredible.

And as these women tend to the altars, they look like they're floating. They radiate. And in the morning, if you're not awake yet (perhaps you're still lying in bed remembering your dreams), you'll wake up to the smell of their trays passing outside of your window. It is so magical, that smell and their dedication to ceremony.

One day, I found an altar and brought it back to San Francisco. I hung it right in my kitchen and tend to it in the morning. When I light the incense, the smell transports me through time and space. Has that ever happened to you? Smell is powerful, and tending to this altar is a very sacred part of my morning routine.

After the altar, I sit down and do morning pages. This is an exercise I learned about in Julia Cameron's *The Artist's Way*. It's three pages of longhand writing. I think she once called it a "brain drain," and that's a really wonderful description of how it feels. It only takes about fifteen minutes, and through the daily ritual of writing, you move mental clutter out of your mind and onto the page. Anything and everything can go onto the page because it's just for you, and even then, Cameron advises waiting six weeks to read what you write. The practice of morning pages is like sweeping the floors—you just feel better afterward.

The final part of my morning routine is reading and writing. Beginning this year, I committed to reading every day for forty-five minutes and responding to that reading for fifteen minutes. I document my writing on note cards, and I hang the cards up in my bathroom and around the studio so I see them all the time. Sometimes I talk to them or imagine they're at a dinner party and seat some cards next to others, and then new ideas come up. It's fun.

Having a morning routine also helped me complete the task of writing a book, and now it's the foundation of my daily practice. When done well, my morning routine takes about two hours. One of my favorite artists, the sculptor Brâncuşi, once said, "It's not difficult to make things. What is difficult is to reach the state in which we can make them." Whether the day is for writing, designing, or painting, the consistent practice of a morning routine is the doorway into it all.

How soon after waking up do you have breakfast?

There's something about being a little bit hungry in the morning that energizes me. Maybe it's a metaphor? But I don't eat a full meal until 1:00 or 2:00 P.M. And when I do, it's breakfast. I love breakfast!

You know that game where they ask what your last meal on earth would be? Mine would be scrambled eggs and pancakes, just like I used to eat as a kid on the weekends. There is this magical little diner that serves breakfast until late in the afternoon, so I often go there. In David Lynch's *Catching the Big Fish*, he says that he goes to the same diner every day and orders a milkshake. I think that's a really nice idea, to go and sit at the same place every day and have a special treat.

For some reason, I imagine he has a lot of good ideas at that diner.

Do you have a morning meditation routine?

My whole morning feels like a meditation. I try to be present to each aspect of my morning routine. There's a lovely story that I heard once that I love:

One day the Buddha was speaking to a prince. The prince asked him, "What do you and your monks do in your monastery?" The Buddha said, "We sit and we walk and we eat." The prince replied, "How are you different, then, from my people, for we do those things as well?" The Buddha responded, "When we sit, we know we are sitting. When we walk, we know we are walking. When we eat, we know we are eating."

LISA CONGDON
Fine artist and illustrator

When your morning routine fuels your creativity
almost as much as your morning coffee.

What is your morning routine?

I wake up every morning at approximately 6:00. Once I'm up I make the bed if it's my turn (my wife and I have a chore chart to make sure we get stuff done around the house, and every other week it's my turn to make the bed), then I meditate for fifteen minutes, get dressed, and go downstairs for coffee. I'm lucky because my wife made a vow to me on our wedding day that she would make me coffee every morning for the rest of my life (as long as she is able). And she's stuck to her promise! So I come downstairs to freshly brewed coffee every day!

I eat a small breakfast, like toast or a little cereal. While I eat, I check email to see if there is anything urgent, and I make my to-do list for the day. Then, several days a week, I head to the gym, swimming pool, or out for a run. Exercise is what really wakes me up and gets me ready for my workday. After my workout, I head back home, get myself dolled up for the day, and get to work. Part of my routine is getting dressed as if I am going to leave my house for my job. My studio is on my property at home, so I don't really leave. But I find that getting dressed in a nice outfit like I would if I was going to an office or retail job helps me feel much better about my day, even though sometimes the only person who sees me is my wife.

How long have you stuck with this routine? What has changed?

This has been my routine since I became self-employed ten years ago.

A couple years ago I moved from San Francisco, California, to Portland, Oregon, which was a big change in my life. This year I added meditation to my morning routine. It was a really tough transition for me to make—having a meditation practice takes enormous discipline when you're tired and groggy in the morning! But I've found that since I started meditating, I'm less anxious and feel happier, with a greater sense of well-being.

What happens if you fail?

Routines are a very important part of being a creative person. I find that when I go off my routine, my sense of balance is skewed. And sometimes that can make me feel really anxious, which, in turn, affects my ability to do good work, or in some cases, to get any work done at all.

My morning routine grounds me and keeps me organized, and that frees me up to focus on making new artwork each day.

YUKO SHIMIZU
Japanese illustrator, instructor at School of Visual Arts

When you intentionally take the local train to work to give yourself five extra minutes of reading time.

What is your morning routine?

I have a real breakfast to start the day, or to break fast, and I make this special vitamin C booster drink to have with it. It involves lots of fresh grated ginger, raw honey, propolis, and half a lemon or lime. In the summer, I add seltzer water to it, which makes it taste like homemade ginger ale. During the colder months, I add lukewarm water (so the good enzymes of the raw honey won't be killed by heat), and it tastes like ginger tea.

My studio is in midtown Manhattan, where there aren't many choices for a good lunch. On top of that, most of the places are overpriced. So, for the past five years or so, I've been bringing lunch from home almost every day. I usually cook a lot of dishes on the weekend that can be frozen and then take them to work to reheat throughout the week. I even steam tons of rice at once and Saran Wrap it in one-meal portions and keep them in the freezer. It's an Asian rice hack that works great. I'll then prepare salads and vegetable dishes in the morning.

To keep myself healthy, I have slowly made lunch the biggest meal of the day. I eat very small dinners nowadays, but my lunch bag is packed with food: sometimes a few days of lunch at a time, so my morning commute often looks like I just went on a big grocery store trip.

I used to read about fifty books a year when I was living in Japan. My school commute was an hour and a half each way. When I started working (I had a corporate office job for eleven years before I moved to New York to go to art school), my commute got shorter, but it was still over an hour. Sadly, phones have changed the commute train scenery in Japan now, but it used to be everyone quietly reading books. Japanese designs for paperbacks are quite remarkable. The size of each book may be half the size of an American paperback, but the paper is super thin and, conversely, super sturdy. Because of the Japanese writing system, they can still keep the font size pretty big.

Now, my time on the subway is only fifteen minutes, and because of phones and tablets, I have lost the habit of reading. In the last few years, maybe I read ten books a year at the most. But to have a creative output, in my case drawings and illustrations, I need creative input, inspirations, and influences. I need to experience things I don't experience on my own. So, the new routine is to finally get back into reading—reading really good books that fuel my creativity.

I now intentionally take the local train instead of switching to the express train as it gives me five extra minutes of reading time per commute (I also use the time I used to waste on my phone to read throughout the day, and especially at night). So far, so good. I am getting a lot of reading done.

What are your most important tasks in the morning?

To relax and enjoy the morning, and to have a good start to the day.

I don't know how people can have a good day when they rush around in the morning. Maybe this two or more hours in the morning is my meditation. Regardless of how crazy the day's schedule is going to be, or even when I know I will have to pull a fourteen-hour workday, I still keep this relaxed morning routine. When I see people who look like they have good jobs eating breakfast from a paper plate on the train platform, I feel sad.

What happens if you're traveling?

I travel a lot, so I know I won't be able to follow the same routine all the time. When I can't, I do my best to find another way to calm and relax myself in the morning.

I've brought lemons and limes onto international flights in the past so I can have my vitamin C drink first thing in the morning. I know you're not supposed to do that, so shhhh. No, I don't do it anymore.

And if you fail?

I have to be flexible, otherwise the routine, which is supposed to relax me, will turn into a stressful event in itself.

DR. JOHN BERARDI
Founder of Precision Nutrition

When you time your morning meditation to
how long it takes your teakettle to boil.

What is your morning routine?

During the week I typically wake up around 7:00 A.M. Most mornings I wake up on my own, however I do have our music system set up to play music starting just after 7:00 in case I need a little encouragement.

After waking, I do a fifteen-minute self-care routine: I go to the bathroom, brush and floss, shave, and take care of my skin (I apply almond oil to my body and use a natural cleanser/scrub/toner/moisturizer on my face). I'll then head into the kitchen, where I prepare breakfast for my wife and four children. Cooking, getting them fed, and getting them into the minivan and off to school takes about an hour.

After my wife and children have left I boil some water for a huge mug of tea. While doing this I sit on the counter next to the teakettle for three to five minutes while the water boils. I'll just sit there with my eyes closed, breathing deeply and clearing my mind. I drink the tea in my home office while I prioritize my work for the day. After about an hour or two I'm done prioritizing and will usually have started my first task. At that point, I take a break for my first meal of the day, after which I work straight through to a late lunch, just before I leave to pick up the children from school.

What time do you go to sleep?

I'm usually asleep by 11:00 or 11:30 P.M., which gives me seven and a half to eight hours of sleep. Truth is, this is just on the border of being too little sleep for me. I usually "catch up" on my slight sleep deficit by getting an extra hour on Saturdays and Sundays.

Do you do anything before bed to make your morning easier?

A few days a week I strength train or do cardiovascular exercise in the evenings, once the kids have all gone to sleep. After the workout, a relaxing shower, and a meal, I'm ready to sleep—though I have to admit that some nights I'll get caught up with reading a book or watching a movie while eating, and get to sleep later.

Do you use any apps or products to enhance your morning routine?

I think the best "app" is the human body. Treat it well with good food, adequate rest, regular exercise, exposure to sunlight, visits to nature, and a good social support network, and things tend to go well.

MELODY McCLOSKEY
CEO of StyleSeat

When cleaning your house and reorganizing in
the morning, against all odds, relaxes you.

What is your morning routine?

I'm an early riser. I like to get up at 5:45 A.M. to give myself some time to think without any distraction. I'll spend about an hour cleaning, or organizing, or dealing with any personal things that need attention. This sounds frivolous, but it's the time I use to process big things, both personal and work related, while doing mundane tasks. At 7:00 I'll work out with a trainer two to four times a week, or I'll be at an exercise class (hot yoga, Pilates, or TRX) most of the remaining days.

How long have you stuck with this routine? What has changed?

I've been getting up early for a few years. For a long period of my life I stayed up very late, but I've since found my early morning routine to be the best way for me to sustain a high output and to feel balanced and happy throughout the day.

Of course, it wasn't easy at first! It was torture getting up that early; I was never naturally a morning person. But now it's become routine, and I wake up pretty early on weekends, too.

What time do you go to sleep?

It depends on whether I'm traveling, what's going on with work, and so on. When I'm in the routine I get into bed around 9:00 P.M., but sometimes it's as late as 10:00 or 11:00. I've started listening to a lot of podcasts before bed. You can hit the sleep button so it stops in ten minutes. It's a good way to make sure I'm falling asleep quickly; if I have to extend the timer more than once I make a note to get more disciplined.

Do you do anything before bed to make your morning easier?

I lay out my workout clothes and set my coffee maker to go off in the morning. Nothing gets me out of bed quicker than the smell of coffee!

Do you use an alarm to wake up?

Yes, and I snooze it all the time, but if I hit snooze I make myself sit up so I don't go back to sleep.

How soon after waking up do you have breakfast?

I eat something small before working out—a piece of fruit, a fried egg with a side of greens. When I get back I usually have a protein shake or some other high-protein meal. Overall I stick to Paleo as much as I can. I've tried a million different diets, and for me, that was the one that really reduced my fatigue and makes me feel the best.

How does your partner fit into your morning?

I'm in San Francisco and my fiancé is in Los Angeles. We don't get as many mornings together as we'd like, but I'm lucky because his morning routine is very similar to my own. When we are apart, we video chat every morning and talk about our days and our upcoming wedding. When we are together, we connect and talk in the mornings, and work out together.

What happens if you fail?

I'm strict about mine because it makes me happy, however, I don't think anyone should feel militaristic about a routine. Do what makes you happy, and when stuff comes up, you can accommodate. I've found the right combo of discipline and cutting yourself a break that nets the best results for me.

AMBER RAE
Author of *Choose Wonder Over Worry*

When your mornings are reserved for accessing inner whispers.

What is your morning routine?

On most days, I wake up without an alarm, put on my workout gear, and head to the Pilates gym down the street for a session with my trainer. I love how he weaves high-intensity training with core work. It kicks my ass every time, and leaves me buzzing with energy.

I then pop by the local grocer for a green juice with lemon, ginger, and cayenne pepper. I grab a stool at their window and dive into morning pages—a stream-of-consciousness writing tool I use for self-connection and accessing inner whispers. Thirty or so minutes later, I have a writing concept or two in the works, and I'm feeling jazzed. I head home for a green smoothie and dance in the living room. The rest of my day is typically open for writing and making art.

How long have you stuck with this routine? What has changed?

I've had variations of this routine—movement, writing, nourishment—for a few years now. Last year, my fiancé and I moved into a loft in Brooklyn, where with my interior designer mom's help we put together an inspiring, creative space. It blends giant Post-it walls with separate analog and digital spaces, a solid speaker system, and a fridge filled with fresh fruits, almond butter, and kale.

When I wake up and look around, it feels like I could be anywhere in the world, which feels grounding in the hustle and bustle of New York.

I recently came across a notebook of mine from about three years ago. At that point in my life I was working around the clock and dating a man, but I didn't feel completely safe in our relationship. In giant letters on many pages I wrote: "OVERWHELMED. OFF-CENTER. NEED TO PRIORITIZE SELF-CARE." For many years, my morning routine was a result of how other people expected me to show up. I was overwhelmed and off-center because I was ignoring the messages my body was sending me. I thought that to thrive in the world of technology and entrepreneurship (the industries I was working in at the time), I must work around the clock, eat lunch at my desk, and wear my lack of sleep like a badge of honor. There seemed to be a high degree of human doing-ness, and I felt a complete void of human being-ness.

So I paused. I slowed down. I started asking myself what rituals and routines supported my creative flow. I got curious about the environments and interactions that led to my greatest work. What I discovered was a natural rhythm of productivity. Thriving was a matter of aligning with and trusting that flow.

For instance, on most days I go to sleep by 2:00 A.M. and rise by 10:30 A.M. I sleep about an hour more in the winter, and enjoy rising earlier in the spring. As a maker, I thrive with large spaces of creation each day, and tend to avoid meetings, phone calls, and technology for long stretches of time. I work best in sprints, so I go all in for days or weeks at a time with pause and recovery in between. My best writing emerges around 11:00 P.M. and ideas tend to flow so long as I'm challenging and inspiring myself.

Initially, stepping into this way of being brought about a sense of guilt. I wondered if I could really take this much ownership of my schedule and I worried what other people would think. What I eventually realized is that we each have a flow that works best for us. What works for me may not work for you. The important thing is to get curious around find-ing your own unique flow, and then creating the space for those around you to do the same.

OVER TO YOU

> "When I'm tempted to skip my morning routine or
> another form of self-care, I remind myself that I can
> better serve the people I love and the projects
> I care about when I start with me."
>
> —COURTNEY CARVER, AUTHOR

When you start your day taking care of your needs you not only access a sense of calm that, whatever the day ahead may hold, can't be taken away from you, you also set yourself up to treat those you meet throughout the day with greater gentleness than you otherwise would have.

As social entrepreneur Jess Weiner notes: "I definitely feel more alive when I've taken time for me, my body, and my relationship . . . My mind feels clear and I feel happier and more energized."

Take heed of our self-care suggestions below:

GIVE YOURSELF "ME TIME" IN THE MORNING

The early mornings are the perfect time to give yourself a short, unabashed dose of "me time" as you can enjoy the quiet of the morning while the rest of the world is still sleeping. Keep in mind that even if you wake up later in the day, or work the night shift, you still have those early hours upon waking within which your "me time" can thrive.

> "I have an extroverted job, I run a company with over 200 employees, and so my time is very much in demand from a professional and personal perspective. My time to myself is very important and rare, so I try to make the most of it."
>
> —JULIEN SMITH, CEO OF BREATHER

You can use this time however you please (this book provides a ton of suggestions for this). Art director David Moore told us: "For too long I worked without properly taking care of myself, and as I've gotten older, it's become apparent that I'm no longer a spring chicken. Eating right, and taking the time to slow down and plan in the morning, is crucial for a productive day."

YOUR MORNING ROUTINE HELPS GROUND YOU

In the words of journalist Tessa Miller: "My morning routine definitely sets the tone for the rest of my day. If I'm rushed and stressed in the morning, that will carry through to my workday. If I have structure and time to get organized, it's usually smooth sailing."

Using your morning thoughtfully allows you to plan for the possibilities of the day to come. It helps you figure out what you really need to get done, and what can fall away, for the time being, in place of more important tasks.

> "If I have a good morning my day is usually great, regardless of what happens throughout it. If I start the day in a bad mood, it makes for a much longer twenty-four hours."
>
> —IAN SARACHAN, SOCCER COACH

Without a routine you're like a ship without a rudder, veering this way and that but never truly sailing the course you've set.

LOOK AT YOUR MORNING FROM ABOVE. WHAT DO YOU SEE?

There is a common exercise in humility in which we are told to visualize our own funeral. What do those attending say about you—do they mention your high-flying career, how you won that client or this award, or how you worked twelve hour days for the best part of your working life? Or do they speak of your character—that is, who you were as a parent, a friend, and a human being?

You can take this same approach to assess how you're currently spending your morning immediately upon wakening. When you look at your morning from above, what do you see? If you've imagined a hurried picture of yourself running from one task to the next as you scroll through the news on your phone and spill coffee down your shirt, consider making a change. Visualize a calmer morning, a gentler morning, a morning in which you put yourself first. And then use all that you have learned in this chapter (and this book as a whole) and make it a reality.

EARLY WINS GIVE YOU A SENSE OF ACCOMPLISHMENT

The early wins that come from having a morning routine (whether getting some pressing work done, or fitting in an early morning workout) help to give you a sense of accomplishment that you can carry into the rest of the day. Director of product management and revenue at Tinder, Jeff Morris,

Jr., notes: "Going to yoga before work has changed my life. When most people are starting to wake up, I already feel like I accomplished something. It's a pretty awesome feeling."

These wins can be a wide variety of things, but their common denominator is the sense of accomplishment you feel after completing them. As author and cofounder of the Rose Park Advisors investment firm, Whitney Johnson, told us: "The thing that has helped me stick to a new routine is realizing that there are so many things that I want to get done. So many. For me, thirty minutes at 5:30 A.M. is equivalent to at least an hour at 3:00 P.M."

REVERSAL

There is no reversal to treating yourself with care and gentleness in the morning.

The one caveat to keep in mind is that you shouldn't fight what works for you, if it is in your best interest. If you tend to get up later in the day and perform your morning routine then, experiment with trying to get up earlier, but if after a couple of weeks the change isn't sticking (and you're not especially interested in seeing it stick), push your wake-up time back again.

CHAPTER 9

DIFFERENT ENVIRONMENTS

Keeping Up Your Routine When
You're Away from Home

THERE'S NOTHING LIKE GETTING AWAY FROM
WORK TO HELP YOU GET MORE WORK DONE

For many of us, sticking to our morning routine when we're traveling is an almost impossible task, something we've tried before but have since concluded isn't going to happen. As a result, we just go with the flow when we're on the road falling out of our regular routine and into some unhealthy habits.

However, it's entirely possible to keep your morning routine in place when you travel, or at the very least to have a travel-ready routine that you always know is there when you need it. Over the next few pages we'll give you ideas on how to do this, whether you consistently find yourself living and working out of hotel rooms, or you just want to be able to keep up your morning routine the few times a year when you're away from home.

In this chapter we'll speak with (among others) author and compulsive traveler Chris Guillebeau, who, despite visiting at least twenty countries a year, insists that his morning routine is key to his creative process; fashion model and cultural activist Cameron Russell on how she works to fit in her morning routine around whatever she's doing (in whatever city she's in) on any particular day; and Bulletproof Coffee's Dave Asprey, whose travel morning routine you'll truly have to see (or rather, read) to believe.

CAMERON RUSSELL

Fashion model and cultural activist

When the only habit your jet-setting lifestyle allows you
to stick to is finding time to read every day.

What is your morning routine?

Every day is totally different. Because I travel a lot for work,
and because my workdays are always different, having a routine really means fitting things in around everything else.

If I have an early call time (any time before 6:00 A.M.) I
usually wake up just five minutes beforehand, pull on clothes,
and dash out. If it's later than that I'll wake up leaving
enough time to have tea, breakfast, and read a few long-form
articles or part of a book.

Reading someone else's writing always feels like a gift. I
adore being inside someone else's thoughtfulness, and half
the time it inspires me to write a little of my own. At this point
I'm usually on my way to work, but I'll write on my phone and
email it to an account I have just for my own writing and notes.

**How long have you stuck with this routine? What has
changed?**

I don't like having a strict routine. I try to make space to read
and write, but I like starting my day with adventure and unpredictability. For example, because of jet lag I'll sometimes
wake up at 4:00 or 5:00 A.M., and my partner and I will take
advantage of our forced early start by going to a new part of
the city to take a long five- to ten-mile walk before our day
begins.

Last spring I spent thirty days writing as soon as I opened my eyes. It was fantastic, and I want to get back to that! I am most productive early mornings and late nights because it's the only time I feel I don't have to be responding to emails, present on social media, or attached in any way to my phone! As an experiment over the summer, I spent two weeks getting up at 5:00 A.M. and going for a run and meditating before work. It felt fantastic, but also not totally realistic for me as a daily practice.

Do you do anything before bed to make your morning easier?

I spend a lot of time living out of a suitcase, which means I've already thought about what I'm going to wear. I like having the flexibility to get up five minutes before I'm supposed to be anyplace and jump right in. I'll save articles to my phone, or read part of a book and dive back in when I wake up. I pretty much always have a to-do list going, so when I get up the next day I know exactly where I should start.

Do you have a morning workout routine?

I like to make space for myself before work. Whenever possible I'll try to have an intellectual or physical adventure before my workday starts. The few times that I've ended up running on a treadmill or going to spin class I've just thought how much more exciting it is to spend this energy and time biking or running through the city.

There is so much freedom when you realize that your own body, without a car or the subway or a bus, can get you someplace far away from where you started.

Do you also follow this routine on weekends?

Yes. I wear a ton of hats, but all as a freelancer. For the past thirteen years I've worked as a model, and I use that background to bring alternative content and culture to the mainstream through multimedia production, mostly with an activist bent. I've written and produced a whole host of multimedia projects on topics ranging from climate change to race to gender equity, and I usually have a couple of projects I'm working on that I fit in between shoot days, weekends, and plane rides. Right now, I'm writing a ton, and working on two short film projects, one about media representation and the other around climate change.

What happens if you fail?

The only routine I really stick to is finding time to read every day. Whether I'm sitting in hair and makeup, or on a plane, the subway, or in a taxi, or just at my desk with tea, reading is a great way to start my day.

CHRIS GUILLEBEAU
Author of *The Art of Non-Conformity*, compulsive traveler

When you love routines, despite your all-go
travel lifestyle requiring a lot of flexibility.

What is your morning routine?

First things first: I'm on the go to at least twenty countries each year, in addition to traveling more than a hundred thousand miles domestically. At the moment, I'm kicking off a thirty-city book tour that has me waking up in a different place nearly every day for five weeks. Therefore, sometimes there's not a routine, or at least the routine varies greatly by time zone.

I was recently in Jakarta, Indonesia, and ended up working a modified night shift for most of the week. I worked on my projects through the night, woke up for a "morning coffee" at 2:00 in the afternoon, and then everything was pushed back from there. It felt a little disorienting because I'd show up at the hotel restaurant for "lunch" around 10:00 P.M., right before they closed for the night. Then I'd have "dinner" during normal breakfast hours before falling asleep as the sun rose.

However, let's talk about my normal routine when I'm home in Portland, Oregon, or at least on the road in the United States or Canada. I try to wake up early, usually around 5:30 or 6:00 A.M. I drink two glasses of water right away. I make my first cup of coffee and spend twenty minutes catching up on the news and seeing if anything urgent came into my inbox or social feeds during the night. Then I make a shift—I shower, head to my office, pick up breakfast along the way, and get down to more "real work."

When I'm writing a book, I try to spend at least two hours every morning working on it. I often have interviews or calls, usually at least one to two times a day and sometimes more, and typically one to two meetings as well. But as much as possible I try to reserve 8:00 to 11:00 A.M. for my own independent work. I drink sparkling water and listen to ambient music while I plow through my list of tasks and projects.

How long have you stuck with this routine? What has changed?

I've settled into it over the past decade or so. Much of that time has also included a lot of active travel. I had a personal quest to visit every country in the world from 2002 to 2013, which required a lot of flexibility, but when I'm home I try very hard to keep to the routine.

What happens if you fail?

The best way to put it is that some failures are acceptable and others aren't. If I've slept poorly or didn't hydrate well, it's a bad omen for the rest of the day. I'll be distracted and unfocused. On the other hand, if I sleep a bit later than usual, it's not always a problem.

Anything else you would like to add?

It may sound like my life is disruptive because of all the travel, but I love routines. Routines help, not hinder, the creative process. I wouldn't be able to produce regular work in multiple fields without being faithful to my routine more often than not.

DAVE ASPREY

Creator of Bulletproof Coffee, biohacker

When you take 120 pills a day in your quest to live to 180 years old.

What is your morning routine?

I'm a night person, but I usually wake up at 7:45 A.M. on school days.

First up, I check to see how I slept the night before to drive awareness of my sleep quality. I have a couple of different apps I use to do that. Then, I make Bulletproof Coffee and breakfast for the family. Yes, both of my school-age kids get about two ounces of Bulletproof Coffee in the mornings to help turn on their brains and give them steady energy throughout the morning. I use a metal filter to preserve beneficial coffee oils, and I mix brewed Bulletproof Coffee with grass-fed butter, Bulletproof Brain Octane Oil, and quite often Bulletproof Collagen Protein. As the coffee is brewing, I take all of my supplements that are best taken on an empty stomach. After my coffee, I take the supplements that are best absorbed with fat.

After breakfast, I take the kids to school. Out of a commitment to my family and peace in the morning, I keep my phone on airplane mode until the kids are dropped off. At this point, I turn on my cell to see if there are any urgent text messages (there rarely ever are).

After the kids are off to school, I start my morning upgrades, which are different, depending on the day. All of this is already on my calendar, so I don't have to think about it. At a minimum, a morning upgrade includes standing on the Bulletproof Vibe for twenty minutes in front of an ultraviolet light to get the benefits of sunlight during the Pacific Northwest winter. (In summer, I'll get my UV rays the old-fashioned way: outside with my shirt off.)

Depending on the day, I will also set aside some extra time for neurofeedback or more exercise. Some days I'll use a machine called Vasper, which gives me about two and a half hours of cardio in about twenty-one minutes, or other days I'll play ping-pong with a ping-pong robot that serves balls really fast, which is a form of brain training that involves movement and increases communication across the left and right brain.

I then start my workday. My day is carefully scripted with every minute scheduled, including "free time," appointments, and time with family. I never have to think about what to do next—it's all on the calendar.

How long have you stuck with this routine? What has changed?

Since my oldest child started school, about five years ago. There was a time before having kids when my morning routine looked wildly different. I would wake up later, I would meditate for an hour, chant—whatever I wanted. But it's important to note that the morning routines of parents are radically different from those of people without kids.

What time do you go to sleep?

I'm a night dweller, and I've found that my best work is produced late at night. I'm far less efficient in the morning—my best workflow ranges between 9:00 P.M. and 2:00 A.M., so I totally endorse staying up later if your body is not ready to shut down and rest just yet.

Do you do anything before bed to make your morning easier?

Sleep is incredibly important to me. I always want to wake up feeling refreshed, and I've taken extra steps to achieve this. One of the easiest ways to get great sleep is to use blackout curtains to keep out all light, and put black tape over small lights on electronics.

What are your most important tasks in the morning?

My most important task isn't just hanging out with my family or taking my kids to school; it's being present with them in the morning. It would be easy to drive the kids to school thinking about work the whole time or checking my phone.

The part for me that requires awareness is being totally present for them, away from work or technology. One way I do this is by telling them a story on the way to school. But this story is special—it's an ongoing one that I've been adding to every morning for the last three years, and the kids are the main characters.

What happens if you're traveling?

There are some definite additions that I make to my routine when I'm traveling. First, if I'm traveling without the kids I usually sleep in a little later, until about 8:30 or 9:00 A.M., depending on what my body needs.

I travel 125 days per year, and let's face it, hotel rooms are full of junk light that can make you weak and tired, as well as crappy, filtered air. The first thing I do when I'm not at home is identify all the blinking, flashing lights in the room and cover them with black tape.

I use my TrueDark (blue light filtering) glasses a lot more when I'm on planes and in hotels, and I make sure to use Sleep Mode (a Sleep Supplement), which has a small amount of bioidentical melatonin to make sure I'm getting quality sleep when I'm in a less than perfect environment. When I wake up in a hotel room, I always open a window so I can get better air and light. Morning light is essential for in-creasing your energy and readying your body and brain for the day.

I take the same number of supplements when I travel, packed in individual baggies. I take about 120 pills every day in my quest to live to at least 180 years old. As for movement when I travel, it turns out that exercise is a physical stressor. So, with the stresses of sleep deprivation, airplane travel, new time zones, and not being in complete control of the quality of my food, my body doesn't need the extra stress of vigorous exercise.

And if you fail?

At this point, I'm not using the routine to deal with stress, I'm using it to maintain resilience and awareness. I'm not reliant on the routine for my performance today; instead, over time the routine builds biological strength and resilience within me.

MELLODY HOBSON

**President of Ariel Investments, chair of the board
of DreamWorks Animation**

When you run a little bit faster on a cold winter's day
because you know a warm, relaxing bath awaits.

What is your morning routine?

Most days I wake up between 4:00 and 5:00 A.M., depending on where I am (I live in Chicago and San Francisco). I set an alarm but I often wake up before it sounds. Before I get out of bed, I check for any urgent emails or news alerts.

I dedicate the beginning of my day to my workout and then to reading newspapers. If I have an appearance on the *CBS Morning Show,* I can wake up as early at 1:00 A.M. PST to begin the process of hair and makeup, as well as any necessary preparation.

How long have you stuck with this routine? What has changed?

Probably more than twenty years. In recent years, I've become a lot more flexible with my wake-up time because I have a small child. Whereas I used to be much more rigid about rising by 4:00 for my workouts, I am now more willing to wait for my daughter to wake up, especially if I've been traveling for work.

How soon after waking up do you have breakfast?

I eat after I work out. I'll typically have two hard-boiled eggs and I drink coffee or tea depending on my mood. This is after drinking two liters of water while I'm exercising.

Can you get into detail about your workout routine?

Yes, but my routine varies based on where I am waking up. Through years of constant traveling, I have been able to develop routines in every major city. I run, lift weights, swim, and spin. If I'm not able to exercise, I feel a bit foggy throughout the day. Rest and exercise are necessary for me to feel 100 percent.

How about morning meditation?

I don't meditate, however my bath time is essential personal time. I take a bath every morning, and use the time to decompress and relax. When I'm running outside on cold days in Chicago, I run faster on the return leg, thinking about my bath.

What are your most important tasks in the morning?

I read physical papers every morning. I like hard copies versus reading online. I read the *New York Times,* the *Wall Street Journal, USA Today,* and recently I have added in the *Financial Times.* If I'm in Chicago, I also read the *Sun-Times.*

How does your partner fit into your morning?

My husband says he "guards the bed" while I am exercising. He and my daughter are usually sound asleep at 4:00 A.M.!

M. G. SIEGLER

General partner at GV (Alphabet Inc.'s venture capital arm)

When your morning isn't complete without
a trusted Starbucks Frappuccino, or three.

What is your morning routine?

I recently moved back to the U.S. from London, so I'm transitioning back to a more normalized schedule. While over there, I would often be doing late-night calls with the U.S., so I typically woke up between 8:00 and 9:00 A.M. and I would quickly check for urgent messages on things that may have happened while I was asleep.

If nothing was too pressing, I would typically read some combination of the *New York Times* or the articles I had saved online the previous day. I would drink a bottled Starbucks Frappuccino while doing this, which some people abhor, including my fiancée. But it's my one vice, something I've done since I was a kid.

At around 10:00 I would dive into email. I liked doing it at this time in the UK because most of the U.S. is still asleep, and therefore not able to immediately respond. I have a deep hatred of email, so I try to do it once a day and ideally not turn it into a back-and-forth volley. This took me to lunchtime, which is when I would usually start my meetings for the day.

How long have you stuck with this routine? What has changed?

In the U.S. my routine is slightly different, largely because I do my email at night instead of in the morning. Again, this is because I like to try to send emails when people can't respond to them immediately!

In the U.S., I typically wake up earlier if I have to head to our office in Mountain View. Or I'll do a meeting or two in the morning. If my schedule is clear, I like to write at this time—but it's rarely clear.

Beyond the U.S./UK differences, I wake up much earlier than I used to. When I was a tech reporter, I would typically work very late into the night, often going to bed around 3:00 or 4:00 A.M. Then I would sleep until 10:00 or 11:00. Seven hours of sleep is my norm, but in those tech-blogging days, I would often get six or sometimes just five hours a night. I sleep much better now. In those days, I would get up and immediately get on my computer to start covering whatever hot story was happening in tech on any given day. I would never eat breakfast, but I still drank that Frappuccino.

How soon after waking up do you have breakfast?

If I have a morning meeting, I'll sometimes have breakfast, but usually it's just me and my Frap.

What are your most important tasks in the morning?

Reading. This is what jump-starts my whole day with ideas and inspiration. I typically read news, but sometimes I'll read a long-form article I have saved.

What and when is your first drink in the morning?

In case it's not clear yet, it's that bottled Frappuccino. I swear, this isn't an ad for Starbucks.

What happens if you're traveling?

I'm bad at this. I'm a creature of habit, so even one difference in the routine (not having the Frappuccino, for example) throws the whole thing off. In some ways, this is a good thing, as it makes me adapt and will occasionally make me realize I should switch up my routine in some way.

PETER BALYTA

President of Education Technology at Texas Instruments

When a childhood spent playing hockey makes
waking up before dawn second nature.

What is your morning routine?

On days when I'm not traveling, I wake up at 5:20 A.M., grab a banana with a glass of water, scan my email to help see what's ahead for the day, and then head out for my daily workout at my local gym.

I'm wired to be disciplined, especially when it comes to fitness. Maybe that comes from when I was a kid in Canada and early morning wake-up calls for hockey practice were a natural part of my routine.

I had been experimenting with running and triathlon training for years, so my mornings used to typically begin with a long run or bike ride. As my job became more demanding and my family—my first priority—grew, it became more difficult to find the extended intervals of time required for triathlon training. I was also getting bored with the repetition, so I got back into martial arts with my kids. But after they earned their black belts, they wanted to pursue other goals. A couple of years ago I found myself with an exercise gap to fill, and that's how I got hooked on my routine. I love it because all it requires is that I walk through the gym door at 5:55 A.M., and the coaches take it from there. We start with a warm-up of light stretching, followed by a high-intensity workout of the day involving constantly changing movements. And that's the beauty of this regimen: the workouts are different every day, similar to the working world, where every day brings new challenges. The idea is to grow your strength, endurance, and conditioning by not allowing your body to get used to the same activity. After a short cool down, I head home.

The house is fully awake when I get back at around 7:00 for breakfast. This is the best part of my day because of all the wonderful conversations we have.

Do you use an alarm to wake up?

I travel a lot, so I set timers every time I sleep. On the road, I make it a point to find time to rest, even in short intervals—especially when I'm working through jet lag.

Can you go into more detail about your workout routine?

Whether I'm at the gym or in a hotel room, I start my mornings with my own "workout of the day"-inspired routine. I love it because it couples physical and mental exercise, and it also allows me to keep to a fitness routine while on the road.

My education is in mathematics and instructional technologies, and my job at TI centers around science and math education, so I use STEM (Science, Technology, Engineering, and Mathematics) skills in my workouts. Not to geek out too much, but I use simple math to determine transition times and physics to determine how to leverage my body around a barbell. Having these skills is especially handy when I'm traveling and don't have a coach at my side. Using both math and physics helps me figure out the best training session for the environment I'm in, and I often bring exercise bands for plyometric and bodyweight movements and use whatever is available in the hotel room—such as a chair—to get my workout of the day in.

Do you use any apps or products to enhance your morning routine?

When I'm at home, I use a noise-canceling speaker next to my bed. Earplugs also help a lot, especially when I'm trying to get some shut-eye on a plane. Add an eye mask and play a white-noise app, and I'm good to go while in transit.

Tell us more about what happens if you're traveling.

My job requires that I travel all over the world. When I'm traveling, I skip the restaurant breakfast to ensure I'm maintaining the same breakfast routine as at home. I've exercised in fully kitted gyms fit for royalty in the UK and outdoor Tai Chi courts in Shanghai with ninety-year-old locals. I still enjoy running to clear my mind, so I actively look for opportunities to squeeze in a run no matter where I am. I've solved a lot of problems in my head while jogging along sections of the Great Wall of China, Munich's Isar River, and the Champ de Mars in Paris. No matter where I am, and regardless of the environment, I use whatever resource is available to exercise.

OVER TO YOU

> "I've fallen off the [productivity] wagon more times than
> a bedraggled Steinbeck drunk in Dust-Bowl America.
> Traveling does that to you."
>
> —WILL PEACH, WRITER

When traveling it can be difficult to keep up your morning routine unless you consciously plan for it ahead of time, and pack your bags and mind accordingly. It helps to have a special morning routine in place, regardless of how similar it is to your at-home routine, that fits your needs while you're on the road.

> "Strangely, I wake up much earlier whenever I'm away from home. I always feel inspired after a productive trip and think that I'm going to be a 'new me' when I get home and wake up every day at the crack of dawn—but I inevitably go back to my old ways within a week."
>
> —JING WEI, ILLUSTRATOR

Here are a few points to take into consideration when you're traveling and staying in a different environment:

WORKING OUT OF A HOTEL ROOM CAN MAKE YOU MORE PRODUCTIVE

This is especially true if you're traveling alone, because when you work from a hotel room you eliminate all your at-home distractions. Andy Hayes, a premium tea seller, notes: "I find hotels to be a great place for quiet, mindful morning moments, as there is no temptation to clean out the refrigerator or reorganize my desk."

If you want to add some familiarity to your morning routine in a hotel room without providing too much of a distraction, consider traveling with an electric kettle or blender so you can make your favorite drink without having to leave your room.

DO SOME SMART SCHEDULING AHEAD OF TIME

Schedule your flights to make sure your morning routine isn't disrupted. Or, if you know you sleep well on planes, schedule them so you travel overnight and land at your destination relatively early in the morning, so you can enjoy an active out-of-doors morning routine from the moment you disembark.

If you know that you never tend to work well in different environments, you may choose not to travel at all when you're in the middle of an important project, instead choosing to protect this time and ensuring that any travel is scheduled for afterward.

MAKE A PLAN AND STICK TO IT

This can be hard to implement on the fly once you wake up in your hotel room, so if you travel a lot it may be a good idea to keep a simple morning routine at all times, that way it won't require much adaptation when you're away from home.

"My schedule is dynamic, so I have to be prepared to adapt. I keep a suitcase packed with thin gym shoes and socks and workout stuff so I can weave that into my schedule when I travel. I'm pretty disciplined about sticking to it."

—KEVIN WARREN, CHIEF COMMERCIAL OFFICER AT XEROX

If you travel only occasionally and therefore want to keep a bulked-up home routine, think about what key habits from your morning routine you can still do on the road, be it meditation, yoga, or light stretching, and plan to include this in your routine when you're away from home.

DON'T BEAT YOURSELF UP

Don't beat yourself up about not perfectly following your morning routine (or even a shortened version of it) while on the road. Whether you're staying in a hotel room alone, or sleeping on a friend's couch, you may find that you're just not as efficient away as you are at home. That's okay.

"Routines are funny things. Following them causes a certain level of stress. Not following them causes a different level of stress. Either way, I'm never totally comfortable."

—STEVEN HELLER, FORMER ART DIRECTOR OF THE *NEW YORK TIMES BOOK REVIEW* AND COCHAIR OF SVA MFA DESIGN PROGRAM

The next time you're planning a trip to stay with friends or relatives, remind yourself of Benjamin Franklin's famous quip from *Poor Richard's Almanack:* "Fish and visitors smell after three days." Get in and out of there as soon as possible, and abide by their morning routine while you're there. Writer Paul French puts this rather wonderfully: "Dawn can be an unforgiving hour to be clattering around in someone else's home. I'll just do what I can without waking people or riling anyone's cat."

REVERSAL

There are a couple of instances on the road when you'll want to throw all notions of following your morning routine out the window in favor of enjoying the here and now. These are:

1. When traveling for important work meetings and events.

2. When traveling for pleasure.

Regarding the first instance, many of the people we spoke with noted that when they are traveling for work, their wake-up time mostly depends on why they're traveling in the first place. And so it should be, especially if you're only away on business for a day or two, and the reason you're away is especially important to your company or career. In this situation, take this time to work as hard as you can, sacrificing all but sleep.

When traveling for pleasure, just go with the flow. Unplug as much as possible on vacation. If you're visiting family members (especially those you don't see very often), enjoy the time you're there with them instead of fretting over your morning routine falling by the wayside.

CHAPTER 10

ADAPTATION

How to Embrace Failure and Adapt to Less-than-Perfect Circumstances

MY MORNING ROUTINE WAS THROWN OFF
SO I JUST STUCK TO THE BASICS

Our mornings rarely go exactly how we want them to. The way we respond to disruptions to our morning routine is more important than the disruptions themselves—if you have a partner, other family members, or roommates to work around in the morning, you may have to forego a few "nice to haves" for the greater good. Embracing nonroutine moments can be especially difficult for perfectionists, so we'll try to chip away at that impulse in this chapter.

Falling off the bandwagon and never getting back on is one of the most common causes of people giving up on their morning routine. With that said, it's completely normal (and encouraged) to want to change your routine from time to time. But this should be done on your terms. When something unexpected comes up during your morning that you absolutely must deal with, you'll want to work with these situations to ensure the rest of your day doesn't suffer unnecessarily.

In this chapter we'll speak with (among others) singer-songwriter Sonia Rao on why she's been playing around with a few different routines to see what works best for her; author and blogger Leo Babauta on why he focuses on keeping his morning routine flexible and intentional; and London-based junior doctor Rumana Lasker Dawood on how working shifts has forced her to be more efficient in the morning.

SONIA RAO

Singer-songwriter

*When you admit to yourself that just because you
can set your own hours, this doesn't mean you should.*

What is your morning routine?

I wake up at around 8:00 A.M. and usually lie there for a moment trying to remember my dream and thinking about the
day ahead. I'll then shower and get dressed. Even though I
work from home most days, I still like to get dressed for the
day right away.

I have breakfast, meditate for thirty minutes, and free-
write for another thirty minutes. At 10:00, I check my email,
social media, and phone. I respond to anything that needs a
reply, then I turn off my phone until evening. (I turn it back
on when I need to call somebody, then I turn it off again.)
Phones drive me crazy—I only feel completely present if
mine is turned off and put away. I know I sound like a weirdo,
but it's made me much happier to keep my phone off for
most of the day.

At 11:00, I do vocal warm-ups, practice violin, and work
for a few hours. This is my favorite part of the day, when I can
put everything out of my mind and focus on music. Right
now I'm preparing for a tour, so I'm working on my live set.
After touring ends, instead of practicing, I'll use this time for
writing new songs.

At 3:00 P.M. I have a late lunch, then from 4:00 to 8:00 or
so, I'll work on the nonmusic parts of being a musician, of

which there are apparently many. When I first started out, I didn't realize how entrepreneurial being a musician would be. I love this other type of creativity, but it does take up quite a lot of time.

How long have you stuck with this routine? What has changed?

This has been my routine for the past couple of years. It changes depending on what phase I'm in. When I was recording my album in Nashville last year, my schedule was much different. When I'm on tour for the next couple of months, I'll be driving and performing almost every day, so it will probably be sleep, drive, play a show, and repeat. I'm really hoping to do some exploring, though, since I haven't been to many of these cities before.

I keep changing it up, playing with different routines to see what feels best. Even though I'm self-employed and could technically set whatever hours I'd like, I've found that I'm most productive and happiest when I stick to the same schedule that most people around me are on. I like to sleep when others are sleeping and have brunch on Sundays like everyone else. When I'm out in the middle of the day on a Wednesday, I start thinking, "Am I doing this whole life thing wrong? Why am I the only person at Trader Joe's right now?" and so on, and I start to question my life choices. To avoid this crisis, I try to stick to a "normal" schedule, for the most part. I used to work at a consulting firm, and when I quit to work on music full time, I thought I would have a nonschedule schedule, writing only when I felt inspired, and so on. But I like showing up to write or practice every day. I think that's what keeps me moving forward, both in terms of my productivity and creativity. I love sitting down at the piano each day and writing whether or not I feel like it. It's the best therapy. Usually the first few songs I write after sitting down are terrible and I throw them out, but then that third song will be one I keep. And it reminds me why the "butt-in-chair" method works, and the cycle continues.

What time do you go to sleep?

Unless I have a show, I'm usually in bed between 11:30 and midnight. When I have a show I'm usually too wired to fall asleep right away, so I'm up later on those nights. I like to read for a while before falling asleep. It's tough for me to transition from being awake to being asleep without focusing my mind on another story.

Do you use an alarm to wake up?

I do. If I get eight hours of sleep, I don't hit the snooze button, but otherwise, I hit it once or twice. Going back to sleep feels too good not to do it.

On tour, after driving and singing so much, I often let my body wake up when it wants, instead of setting an alarm. It's really important to me to stay healthy and feel good on tour. I want to enjoy it, not struggle through it.

Do you have a morning workout routine?

No. I always wanted to be that kind of person, but I hate it. I took a morning spin class once, but it's so awful. This extremely cheerful person is yelling at you to bike faster, and it's 7:00 A.M., and it's all terrible. I haven't been back.

What and when is your first drink in the morning?

I drink a glass of water and then a cup of chai. I drink two more cups of chai as the day goes on. Many more if I'm writing songs that day. If not, I switch to decaf tea.

Can you tell us more about your on-tour routine?

I love to feel steady and grounded, but with music there is a lot of unpredictability and travel. I think that's why I create a schedule for myself when I am at home. It gives me a sense of rhythm.

When I'm on tour for the next couple months, I'll be moving between thirty-four cities and I want to feel steady somehow. I will definitely write and meditate each morning; besides these two things, though, I'll leave the rest unscheduled. The shows are already so scheduled, so I want to use whatever time is left over to explore the cities I'm in, and write new songs.

AUSTIN KLEON

Author of *Steal Like an Artist*

When your biggest task is trying to keep your headspace
from being invaded by the outside world.

What is your morning routine?

MORNING ROUTINE

- COFFEE + BREAKFAST
- 3 MILE WALK WITH WIFE (AND DOG & KID IN STROLLER)
- SHOWER
- MEDITATE
- WRITE / MAKE POEM
- EMAIL, TWITTER, ETC.

How long have you stuck with this routine? What has changed?

Ever since my first son was born. The luxury of working from home and not having a job-job is that we're able to wake up slowly and take our time easing into the day. There's no frantic rush to get in the car and get somewhere. And since we get up so early, I'm usually at my desk not that much later than when I worked at an agency.

How soon after waking up do you have breakfast?

Right away. We usually eat some eggs or peanut butter toast and a smoothie or, when we're feeling decadent, breakfast tacos.

Do you have a morning workout routine?

Almost every single morning, rain or shine, my wife and I load our two sons into a red double stroller (we call it the War Rig) and we take a three-mile walk around our neighborhood. It's often painful, sometimes sublime, but it's always *essential* to our day. It's when ideas are born, when we make plans, when we spot suburban wildlife, when we rant about politics, when we exorcise our demons.

We almost never miss this, and I consider it the most important part of my day. I don't take morning meetings or go to morning meetups or whatever because it would mean I'd miss this walk.

What are your most important tasks in the morning?

The biggest task is to try to keep my headspace from being invaded by the outside world, to be alone with my own thoughts before I can sit down and make something.

What and when is your first drink in the morning?

My brother-in-law ruined my life and taught me what good coffee is and how to make it. It's a ritual: turn on the kettle, grind the beans, rinse the filter, brew.

What happens if you fail?

I try to forgive myself and move on. (Sun comes up, sun goes down. Always another chance tomorrow.) One thing about a routine is that the days when you break it can be some of the most interesting days. The routine days make the off-routine days even sweeter (like having a donut on a sugar-free diet), but they wouldn't unless you had a routine to break.

RUMANA LASKER DAWOOD
Junior doctor, dressmaker

When your crazy day job has the surprising benefit of teaching you to roll with the punches in your morning routine.

What is your morning routine?

My first alarm of the day is for morning prayers, which are at around 3:00 A.M. at this time of the year. When this alarm goes off I need to shoot straight out of bed and avoid hitting the snooze button, otherwise I'll sleep right through it. We normally pray in the dark—there's something jarring about having lights on at that hour. It takes us around ten minutes to complete our prayers before we clamber back into bed.

My main alarm goes off at 6:20, but this time I'll hit the snooze button two times (three, if I know what I'm going to wear) before actually getting out of bed. Then I'm go-go-go:

teeth, shower, face, before quickly ironing some clothes and wrapping my hijab. I have a rough idea of how long all these things take me and can gauge whether I can fit in a bowl of muesli. This is my moment of peace, sitting down and catching up with the news headlines on my phone before rushing out of the house.

How long have you stuck with this routine? What has changed?

My day job as a doctor means that my shifts vary from day to day, and every six months when I change the ward/specialty I'm working in. So each day is a slight variation of this.

Over the years I've managed to streamline my morning routine. I definitely cut out a good chunk of the morning when I started wearing a hijab. It was great when I no longer needed to spend that time taming my hair in the mirror! Instead I converted that time into sleep—if I don't get a good night's rest I will feel it the next day.

Do you have a morning workout routine?

On one particular job where my shifts started later in the day, I tried to move my exercise routine to the morning. But I felt so exhausted and couldn't really handle the "burn" kicking in in the middle of the shift, so I switched back to evening workouts!

How does your partner fit into your morning?

My husband is also a doctor, so it varies with his shifts. Most of the time one of us starts a lot earlier than the other, so we don't really get in each other's way.

What happens if you fail?

I'm a really "routine" person, and so if something goes out of sync it can really throw me and make me feel flustered. But I've learnt from my day job to expect the unexpected and roll with it, so once I'm at work I just get back into the swing of things.

DANIEL EDEN
Product designer at Facebook

When you actually like the forced headspace of your morning commute.

What is your morning routine?

I wake up at 6:30 A.M. with an alarm. I keep my phone across the bedroom, in a futile effort to get me out of bed in the morning. At twenty seconds past 6:30, I crawl back into bed, phone in hand, and sleepily check email and social media for half an hour. I'll then take a quick shower, get dressed, and open my laptop, triaging emails and messages until it's time to walk to the shuttle that takes me to Facebook's campus.

The shuttle ride is usually around an hour, and I often spend that time either working on a generative art piece, reading, or simply watching the roads. People gripe or wonder about the commute, but I like the forced headspace it can foster.

My routine on Wednesdays is a little different. I tend to work from home on Wednesdays, so I get up at the same time, but rather than leaving for Menlo Park, I walk around the block, buy my girlfriend and me some coffee and breakfast, walk back to my apartment, and loudly play music as I settle into focusing on tactical work. The project I'm currently working on requires an extra dose of creativity and novel ideas, so I'm occasionally trying to inject some of the Wednesday morning essence into the other weekday routines.

What time do you go to sleep?

I try to make sure I'm in bed by 10:30 P.M. I recently made all the lights in my house "smart," and something nice enabled by that has been setting up my lights to dim to "off" between 10:00 and 10:30. Sitting in the dark on my phone is a helpful reminder to go to bed.

Do you do anything before bed to make your morning easier?

I've started showering before bed, which has helped me feel more refreshed before I sleep. I don't know if it's helped my morning routine, but feeling fresh certainly helps me fall asleep faster.

How does your partner fit into your morning?

My girlfriend is much more morning oriented than I am. She often wakes up egregiously early—we're talking 5:30 A.M.—and goes for a run around Lake Merritt before I even wake up. She's definitely made me more of a morning person. We both enjoy an early night and getting things done early in the morning.

YOLANDA CONYERS

Chief diversity officer at Lenovo

When finding that delicate balance between
work and play doesn't come easily.

What is your morning routine?

I balance structure and flexibility in my morning routine. As a leader in a global company who works remotely, I often have calls starting as early as 7:00 A.M. from colleagues in Asia. That means I'm usually awake by 6:30. Once I'm up I'll grab my morning snacks, and between 7:00 and 10:00 I juggle work calls, replying to email, and eating breakfast.

I always schedule a break in my calendar at 10:00 for my workout. I love hiking near my home—getting out in nature helps to ground and energize me. I'll hike three times a week, four if I incorporate the weekend. In fact, my husband often hikes with me now that he is retired. In a busy household balancing family and work, it's our chance to connect and make sure we're spending important quality time with each other. When I'm hiking alone, I listen to an eclectic mix of music, from Bruno Mars to Beyoncé to Marvin Gaye.

How long have you stuck with this routine? What has changed?

I joined Lenovo ten years ago as a remote employee. At the beginning, it was an adjustment to work outside of a traditional office environment. I worked constantly. Part of this was being new to the company, so I was learning, but another part of it was because I didn't know how to balance my time. I had never worked remotely before, and it took me a couple of years to figure out how to carve out time for myself and not feel guilty about it. I had to realize that when I travel globally and my weekend is taken away to travel, I deserve that time back. It is never perfect, but I reconcile that when I'm home, it is okay for me to spend time on just me and my family.

Working remotely is challenging because you're never really off the job. I have to consciously decide to take a break and do the things I need to do in my personal life and not feel guilty about taking an hour out of the day to see my son run in a track meet. By having a loose structure each day, prioritizing what I need to accomplish with work and with my family, and by being flexible, I can effectively balance both of these demands.

Do you have a morning meditation routine?

I don't do formal meditation, but I pray on my hikes. My hikes are a form of mental de-stressing. Surrounding myself in nature is inspiring and reminds me that the world is so much bigger than myself, and this is God's creation.

LEO BABAUTA
Creator of Zen Habits

When you try to spend your mornings the same way you want to spend your whole life.

What is your morning routine?

I don't have a fixed routine anymore. Lately I've just been trying to make sure that my mornings are 1) intentional, 2) focused on important work, and 3) flexible. That usually means I meditate, have coffee, and write. But I might also read or do yoga, and spend time with my wife. Generally, I try to be awake by 6:30 A.M., but sometimes it's 7:00 or even later, depending on when I get to sleep.

How long have you stuck with this routine? What has changed?

I've been doing some version of this flexible, intentional "no-routine" morning routine for a few years now. It changes all the time, to be honest. I used to be much more rigid with my morning routine, and much more focused on productivity. Now I'm more focused on mindfulness and not being rigid. Every day is different, and I try not to be bothered by that.

Can you tell us more about morning meditation?

I usually meditate first thing in the morning. I meditate in the Zen style, which starts with breath meditation and then objectless meditation (shikantaza). I keep it simple.

How does your partner fit into your morning?

My wife and I usually have coffee together and read. She gives me my space to do my routine, and I give her space to do hers.

What happens if you fail?

My routine isn't fixed, there really aren't days when I don't follow it. But there are days when things go sideways for various reasons. My practice when this happens is to mindfully check in with myself whenever I can, and remember what's important.

Anything else you would like to add?

I try to spend my mornings like I want to spend my whole life: mindfully, flexibly, and with compassion. I'm not perfect at any of it.

ANA MARIE COX
Political columnist and culture critic

When you have to remind yourself that some days,
simply getting out of bed is a victory.

What is your morning routine?

I get up between 7:00 and 7:30 A.M., though I'm always planning on getting up earlier. I pray and set an intention for the day. If I have time, I'll do a five-minute meditation and morning pages. Ideally, I'll have waited until after the meditative stuff to check my phone to make sure nothing has blown up, literally or figuratively. If things are relatively normal, I make my coffee (a ritual unto itself) and read something not on a screen for twenty to thirty minutes. If things are not normal, if there's some huge story that will overtake my day anyway, I'll turn on the TV and start reading up on it online.

Do you do anything before bed to make your morning easier?

I say an evening prayer and remind myself of my intention for that day. I also set out my journal, with a pen, for the following morning.

How does your partner fit into your morning?

Ha! My husband sleeps in a bit later than I do. I have to ask him not to bother me if I'm meditating or writing. General rule: headphones in = do not disturb. If he's up and about when I'm doing my morning reading, we might turn on the TV and watch some news together over coffee.

Anything else you would like to add?

When I read other people's routines in this kind of roundup, I always compare them to mine, and always find my own discipline lacking. It gives me lots of delicious new reasons to beat myself up—Oh, she runs a mile! He reads the whole front section of the *New York Times*! She dispenses with her entire email queue! I'd like anyone reading this to know these things are always aspirational! I've battled depression from time to time, and in those periods, I've needed to remind myself that simply getting out of bed can be a victory. What we are capable of changes from day to day, and it's important to recognize and honor that—it means celebrating yourself for what you were able to do that day.

When you come up with a morning routine, understand that you're undertaking it in order to do something good for yourself, not to meet some stranger's standard of productivity. This is why prayer is such an important part of my routine—and probably the only thing, next to coffee, that I never fail to include. Prayers remind me that today is a gift, no matter how I use it. It is a gift to wake up another day, to have another chance to work toward being the person I was set on this earth to be. Running a mile before breakfast and Instagramming my avocado toast isn't necessarily a part of that.

OVER TO YOU

> "There is enormous power in nailing your morning routine,
> but there's even more power in adapting to it
> when it doesn't happen as we'd like. Routine aids us in
> being our most productive, but change helps us expand
> our comfort zone. Both are positive."
>
> —TERRI SCHNEIDER, ENDURANCE ATHLETE

Embracing nonroutine moments in your morning routine is a way of looking at the hand you've been dealt, brushing it off, and realizing that, underneath, you can still work with it.

Rather than thinking of these moments as failures, it's important to remember that your routine is a means to an end, not the end itself. If you allow the failure to follow certain parts of your routine to creep in and affect the quality of not just the rest of your morning, but the rest of your day, your routine is not really doing what it's supposed to be doing in the first place.

> "I used to allow missing an aspect of my routine to negatively impact my whole day. I now see life as a continual fluctuation of routine, with change being the only constant. If I fail, I know that I need to take away one or two layers of my routine, and get down to the basic pillars: good sleep, a mindful start, and exercise and water."
>
> —JOEL GASCOIGNE, CEO OF BUFFER

When you embrace your less-than-perfect circumstances and allow yourself to adapt to them, you're guarding your morning routine against spinning off course when you come up against similar situations in the future, and in turn you're making your routine more robust. When we asked General Stanley McChrystal what the limfac, or limiting factor, of his morning routine is, he noted that it's usually something outside of his control, such as a client wanting to do an early breakfast meeting. When this happens, he chooses to simply get up earlier to complete his morning routine ahead of the early meeting. He adapts the timing of his routine to still get it in. It's not ideal, but it allows his morning routine to hold up and adapt to the change.

Don't let your morning routine fall apart at the first sign of stress. Learn how to embrace nonroutine moments in your mornings:

WHEN YOUR MORNING ROUTINE FEELS LIKE IT'S FALLING APART, STICK TO ONE OR TWO KEY THINGS

Sometimes, through no fault of your own, your morning starts to feel like it's crashing down around you. We all know the feeling of stress and frustration this brings—when this happens, take it upon yourself to stick to, and complete, just one or two core parts of your morning routine.

This may be your workout, or it may be your meditation session, or it may just be sitting down to spend five minutes with your child before you head out the door. When you start to go off track, make a plan and stick to it. Regroup and stay in control instead of letting your morning fall apart.

"Not everything goes according to plan, but it's usually not the end of the world. If something derails my typical routine, I try to get the most important tasks done more than other miscellaneous ones. I just have to prioritize, then all is well."

—CAT NOONE, CEO OF IRIS HEALTH

You may decide that it's easier to have shorter versions of your routine in place, should you go off track. Instead of fitting in your full workout routine, for example, you may choose to do some light yoga stretches instead. If you can't sit for your standard ten-minute meditation, go ahead and reduce it to five. Other ways to get back on track include getting outside briefly, walking, standing up and stretching, jumping up and down, and breathing deeply.

FAILURE COULD BE A SIGN THAT YOUR ROUTINE NEEDS A SHAKE-UP

If you find that you keep failing to do a certain part of your morning routine, this could mean that this particular item needs to be adapted or removed.

As writer and designer Patrick Ward told us: "If I start failing to do a certain part of my routine, this is usually a sign that I need to change things up. No routine will work forever so I always keep an eye out for ways I can improve my routine or make it more efficient."

Figure out what went wrong (what you failed to do), why it went wrong, and then work from there. You may find that factors not connected to the item itself were at play. Perhaps you've been extra tired recently, or perhaps you are no longer invested in the item itself or simply are no longer enjoying it. If this is the case, drop it.

EMBRACE THE CHALLENGE OF SUCCEEDING DESPITE THE CIRCUMSTANCES

On the opposite end, you shouldn't give up on your failures too easily.

As writer and long-distance swimmer Sarah Kathleen Peck recalls: "In college, I had a major swimming competition coming up, and for reasons outside of my control, I didn't sleep the night before, as I'd had major asthma attacks all night from chemical imbalances in the pool in Chicago. I went to my coach the next morning, haggard, and said, 'I feel TERRIBLE.' He told me to lie down for thirty minutes and to visualize that I'd gotten the best rest of my life, and that it was a champion day, and then come back."

"When I came back he said, 'Here's the thing. If you had perfect circumstances, you could own this race. You could win. The bigger challenge is winning even when you're down—even when you're fatigued. Get out there and fight, despite the circumstances.' He taught me that no one has perfect circumstances, and you're allowed to go on and do incredible things even if you're not feeling perfect about it. Often we get so wedded to a routine that we forget that things can all go haywire and you can still do an incredible job."

If a certain part of your morning routine really isn't working for you, then you should adapt or remove it, but if you've been thrown a tough situation, this is your chance to rise up to meet the challenge.

WHEN IT COMES TO YOUR PARTNER, COMPROMISE IS KEY

Finding harmony between your routine and your partner's is crucial to setting both of you up for a good morning. This especially holds true if you and your partner are on mismatched sleep schedules. Being in a relationship with someone on a different sleep schedule than yours is common, and while making that compromise is never easy (and is always going to result in you both feeling sleepy at some point in your day), it's more than worth it to spend more time with your partner.

Steven Heller told us that his morning is like a cartoon version of life: "My wife goes one direction, I go the other, and we meet in the kitchen." If you wake up earlier than your partner, consider waiting until they're awake (if your schedule allows) to have breakfast together, or go for a walk together, or even head out on an early morning workout together.

REMEMBER THAT TOMORROW IS A NEW DAY

Tomorrow is a new day. If you failed to follow your morning routine today, that's okay.

In the words of author and speaker Crystal Paine: "I have a choice: I can choose to beat myself up over the fact that I am not following my usual routine, or I can give myself grace. I'm working on doing a better job of giving myself grace—because life happens and it's okay if we don't always do everything we'd hoped or planned to do. The best thing I can do on those days is to remind myself to just do what I can."

REVERSAL

There is a clear reversal to this. What if, instead of just embracing nonroutine moments in your morning routine, you actively sought them out? Or, at the very least, you jumped on them when they arrived?

Manuel Lima notes: "Routines are like any set of rules. They can be helpful in giving us a sense of constancy, but at times, breaking them can be extremely liberating. Being a slave to a single routine can prevent spontaneity and unexpected discoveries."

Do you become bored if something is the same (potentially even "too" routine) every day? Consider creating a few different routines that you can choose from each morning. Focus on not being rigid. Shake things up from time to time, and have fun with it.

CONCLUSION

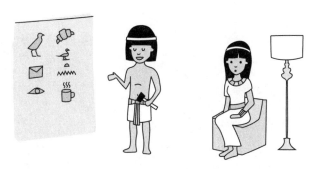

I'M WRITING OUT MY IDEAL MORNING ROUTINE

If you take anything from this book, remember to experiment. Copy something that caught your eye, experiment, adjust, experiment some more, adjust some more, and watch yourself loving new things you never even thought you'd try.

Like every new skill, mastering your morning routine will take some time. Review any notes or highlights you made while reading this book, and follow our simple process:

1. Write down your new routine. Be as specific as necessary. (For example, "go to the bathroom" may not require further detail.)

2. Use waking up as the trigger to begin your morning routine, with each subsequent element of your routine reminding you to start on the next element.

3. Start small—a five-minute workout is less intimidating than a half-hour session.

4. Give yourself small rewards after completing the hardest parts of your routine.

5. Give each new element you bring into your morning routine a fair shot. Trying something for just a couple of days before giving up isn't enough. Though opinion varies on how long it takes for something to become a habit, we suggest you give each new element at least a one- or two-week trial to see how you like it.

Take heart from the successes and failures in this book. The individuals we spoke with have been honest about what works and what doesn't work for them, and, just like you, they've had to figure everything out along the way. And if they're anything like us, they're still experimenting with tweaking, changing, and optimizing their routines in an attempt to bring greater results still.

Don't feel like you must change your morning routine all at once. If there's anything that will doom your efforts before you even begin, this is it. When you add or subtract a new habit, let it be one at a time. Pretend you're a one-year-old who hates change, and treat yourself with that level of gentleness.

Remember, you will constantly come up against obstacles when attempting to stick to your new morning routine—the main offender being the siren call of laziness. Don't let your old routine get a look in. Anyone who has ever tried to change anything about themselves has come up against these same roadblocks. The only way to get through them is to face them head on, to stay flexible, and to not see one solitary missed day as a setback. Remember the bigger picture, and get back to your new routine tomorrow.

The act of staying accountable in this context doesn't just mean staying accountable to your morning routine, but rather staying accountable to yourself. Why did you want to improve your morning routine in the first place? What were you looking to get out of it? The ability to stick to your morning routine over the long term, even when it's hard, takes time to cultivate. Yet we all have the capacity to stay accountable to ourselves—and we encourage you to use it.

Trust the process. This means doing the same things over and over again. It's not exciting, but it is real, and it is life changing.

STATISTICS

For the curious reader, here is a breakdown of the statistics taken from our interviews with more than 300 people (53% female, 47% male) about their morning routines.

7:29 h	**6:24 a.m.**	**10:57 p.m.**
Sleep avg.	Wake-up avg.	Bedtime avg.

The early birds we spoke with start their day as early as 3:00 A.M., while some of the late risers sleep in past 9:00. By 8:30, 97% of the people we interviewed are up.

70%	Use an alarm	**39%**	Same routine on weekends
33%	Snooze	**56%**	Can follow routine anywhere

Thirty-eight percent of our interviewees sleep 8 hours a night, followed by 35% who sleep 7 hours, and 14% who sleep just 6.

54%	Meditate	**48%**	Check email immediately
78%	Exercise	**60%**	Check phone immediately

As for breakfast, more than half (53%) of the people we interviewed have fruit for breakfast, but eggs (40%), oatmeal (33%), toast and other forms of bread (32%), and smoothies (21%) are also firm favorites. Fifty-seven percent of our participants drink water first thing in the morning, but coffee (29%) and tea (8%) are also popular choices.

ACKNOWLEDGMENTS

We are thankful to everyone we interviewed for this book both for their time and for their willingness to share details of this most intimate time of day with us. We're also thankful to everyone we quoted in this book, as well as those we have interviewed for our website over the past five years. Needless to say, this book would not have been possible without you.

We're immensely grateful to Leah Trouwborst, our editor at Portfolio/Penguin, for believing in this book as an idea, and for working with us in partnership for almost two years to make it a reality. It would never have come to light without her. At Portfolio we would also like to thank Helen Healey, Aly Hancock, Rebecca Shoenthal, Taylor Edwards, Margot Stamas, Will Weisser, Niki Papadopoulos, and Bria Sandford for their hard work and continued belief in our book, and we would like to give a most sincere thank-you to Adrian Zackheim for giving us a shot in the first place.

We're grateful to Tim Wojcik, our agent. Thank you for writing the opening paragraph of this book twelve months before we attempted to better it (we could not). Thanks also to our copyeditor, Jane Cavolina; our UK editor, Lydia Yadi; and our website editor, Michele Boltz. Thank you to Liz Fosslien, who expertly illustrated the cartoons within the pages of this book, and to Benjamin's wife, Audra Martyn Spall, for her detailed comments on the manuscript at every step of the way. Her diligence and insight improved the book immensely, and for that we are very grateful.

Finally, we would like to thank everyone who has followed along, read our interviews, and in any way contributed to the conversation over the past five years. This book is for you.

SELECTED BIBLIOGRAPHY

Aurelius, Marcus. *Meditations: A New Translation*.

Currey, Mason. *Daily Rituals: How Artists Work*.

Franklin, Benjamin. *Autobiography*.

Duhigg, Charles. *The Power of Habit*.

Holiday, Ryan. *The Obstacle Is the Way*.

Webb, Caroline. *How to Have a Good Day*.

Newport, Cal. *Deep Work*.

Seneca. *Letters from a Stoic*.

Harris, Dan. *10% Happier*.

Hesse, Hermann. *Siddhartha*.

Yogananda, Paramahansa. *Autobiography of a Yogi*.

Huffington, Arianna. *Thrive*.

Thoreau, Henry David. *Walden*.

Ferriss, Tim. *Tools of Titans*.

Lamott, Anne. *Bird by Bird*.

Cameron, Julia. *The Artist's Way*.

Allen, James. *As a Man Thinketh*.

SHARE AND STAY INSPIRED

Now it's your turn to step up. We would love to hear about your new morning routine. Share a photo of it (or any part of it) on Instagram, Twitter, or Facebook using the #mymorningroutine hashtag.

Wake up! I want to show you my new #mymorningroutine

Want to get a brand new morning routine in your email inbox every week? Join our free newsletter by going to mymorningroutine.com/newsletter and we'll see you again soon!